流动的杂货摊
mobile street vendor

竹编师傅的脚踏车
bamboo-weaving master's bicycle

坐
垫
开
NO
P

弹棉花师傅的脚踏车
cotton-fluffing master's bicycle

Zhou Qi
Shanghai
Shifu
(Master)
Memories of Vanishing
Handicrafts
上海人民美術出版社

上海师傅
最后的手作记忆
周祺

感谢：蔡英龙、陈天星、陈志刚、储进根、丁维昌、费宝英、甘丽娟、顾玲娣、顾月香、顾振邦、郭志高、何永娣、华雪娟、黄达明、黄发堂、黄金善、居台仁、李建国、李政、凌旭明、马根发、浦阿婆、秦师傅、唐师傅、沈木云、沈友高、孙逸娟、陶情建、王根林、王宏春、王全林、王秀丽、王雪根、魏鹏飞、吴德华、吴孝明、夏耀明、徐冬林、徐建章、徐巧珍、徐文鸿、许文明、薛文华、杨秋玲、杨慎喜、杨忠岐、殷允良、俞锦仙、俞文归、查沛华、张凤仙、张福平、张乐华、赵士德、朱阿梅、朱金林、周宏梅、周万德、周伟清、庄金生

白杰、蔡祺、陈丹燕、曹可欣、陈琪、陈幼坚、都筑响一、段段、方叙洁、冯美丽、高秀娟、顾未妹、顾铮、郭允、韩峰、韩天红、横井邦弘、胡惠萍、胡卫娣、胡文杰、洪人杰、黄斌、黄永松、金宇澄、井磊、李钧鹏、李恺、李明洁、梁瀚杰、林清、刘大泓、刘昊星、刘明泉、陆君玖，陆萧、陆元敏、陆忠华、罗英、马德岗、马可·赫尼格、马神龙、倪卫华、潘慧、庞晶晶、清水耕助、瞿玉珠、儒雅德、深泽直人、沈熙荣、沈月明、盛雪娟、孙亚、唐骋华、唐昊君、唐晖、唐凌洁、汤惟杰、唐卫英、田兆元、屠爱军、王桂芳、王竞、王静雯、温泽远、吴南瑶、吴越、席闻雷、谢晓啸、许贝贝、许昊旸、徐华、许丽英、徐勤、宣晓翊、盐野米松、杨帆、杨晓晖、殷恬静、英珂、原研哉、俞晓菁、余友涵、袁佳青、张翠、张根芳、张洪英、张磊、张少俊、张淑伶、张雯茜、张渊、周蓓丽、周浩、周慧玲、周宇平、中田美佐、钟子平、诸皓、朱丽珏、竹村信之、朱玲玲、朱金娥

特别感谢上海人民美术出版社社长顾伟先生，总编辑邱孟瑜女士，及本书的美术指导姜庆共先生，责任编辑张瓔女士的鼓励和指教

感谢我的家人，周玉麟，张仁凤，周康华，林培君，在生活和工作上给我很多的启发、支持、教育和爱

Thanks: Cai Yinglong, Chen Tianxing, Chen Zhigang, Chu Jin'gen, Ding Weichang, Fei Baoying, Gan Lijuan, Gu Lingdi, Gu Yuexiang, Gu Zhenbang, Guo Zhigao, He Yongdi, Hua Xuejuan, Huang Daming, Huang Fatang, Huang Jinshan, Ju Tairen, Li Jianguo, Li Zheng, Ling Xuming, Ma Genfa, Ms. Pu, Mr. Qin, Mr. Tang, Shen Muyun, Shen Yougao, Sun Yijuan, Tao Qingjian, Wang Genlin, Wang Hongchun, Wang Quanlin, Wang Xiuli, Wang Xuegeng, Wei Pengfei, Wu Dehua, Wu Xiaoming, Xia Yaoming, Xu Donglin, Xu Jianzhang, Xu Qiaozhen, Xu Wenhong, Xu Wenming, Xue Wenhua, Yang Qiuling, Yang Shenxi, Yang Zhongqi, Yin Yunliang, Yu Jinxian, Yu Wengui, Zha Peihua, Zhang Fengxian, Zhang Fuping, Zhang Lehua, Zhao Shide, Zhu Amei, Zhu Jinlin, Zhou Hongmei, Zhou Wande, Zhou Weiqing, Zhuang Jinsheng

Alan Chan, Cai Qi, Chen Danyan, Cao Kexin, Chen Qi, Connie Chang, Duan Duan, Fang Xujie, Feng Meili, Gao Xiujuan, Gu Weimei, Gu Zheng, Guo Yun, Han Feng, Han Tianhong, Henry Chung, Hu Huiping, Hu Weidi, Hu Wenjie, Hong Renjie, Huang Bin, Huang Yongsong, Jake Newby, Jin Yucheng, Jing Bartz, Jing Lei, John Sunyer, Katherine Hulling Chou, Kenya Hara, Kimi Tang, Kouske Shimizu, Kyoichi Tsuzuki, Li Junpeng, Li Kai, Li Mingjie, Liang Hanjie, Lin Qing, Liu Dahong, Liu Haoxing, Liu Mingquan, Lu Junjiu, Lu Xiao, Lu Yuanmin, Lu Zhonghua, Luo Ying, Ma Degang, Ma Shenlong, Marcus Hernig, Misa Nakata, Naoto Fukasawa, Ni Weihua, Pan Hui, Pang Jingjing, Qu Yuzhu, Ruard William Absaroka, Shen Xirong, Shen Yueming, Sheng Xuejuan, Takemura Nobuyuki, Tang Chenghua, Tang Haojun, Tang Lingjie, Tang Weijie, Tang Weiying, Tian Zhaoyuan, Tu Aijun, Wang Guifang, Wang Jingwen, Wen Zeyuan, Wu Nanyao, Wu Yue, Xi Wenlei, Xie Xiaoxiao, Xu Beibie, Xu Haoyang, Xu Hua, Xu Liying, Xu Qin, Xuan Xiaoyi, Yang Fan, Yang Xiaohui, Yin Tianjing, Ying Ke, Yokoi Kunihiro, Yonematsu Shiono, Yu Xiaojing, Yu Youhan, Yuan Jiaqing, Zhang Cui, Zhang Genfang, Zhang Hongying, Zhang Lei, Zhang Shaojun, Zhang Shuling, Zhang Yuan, Zhou Beili, Zhou Hao, Zhou Yuping, Zhu Hao, Zhu Lijue, Zhu Lingling, Zhu Jin'e

Special thanks to the president of Shanghai People's Fine Arts Publishing House Mr. Gu Wei and the chief editor Ms. Qiu Mengyu, As well as the art director of this book Mr. Jiang Qinggong, editor-in-charge Ms. Zhang Ying

Thanks to my families for their inspiration, support, education and love in life and work, namely Zhou Yulin, Zhang Renfeng, Zhou Kanghua and Lin Peijun

注：本书摄影、插画 周祺
照片内字迹为师傅本人手写
物件解释选自《上海话大词典》等

Notes: photography, illustration by Zhou Qi
the words on the photos are written by Shifu
definitions of objects quoted from Shanghai Dialect Dictionary and others

目录

Contents

detachable collars

019 detachable collar

Xu Donglin: I used to have 27 apprentices

020 cake barrels

Wei Pengfei—The eldest bamboo weaving Shifu

021 bamboo steamers

Gu Lingdi: This used to be the street for Mie Bamboo and every shop sold bamboo wares

022 hand-held basket

023 bamboo hat

024 bamboo hanger

025 bamboo clip

Sun Yijuan: In the 1970s, we got a lot of export orders

026 straw bag

027 straw hat

028 straw slippers

029 cup holder

030 candy box basket

Zhao Shide—Bamboo artisan who both makes and sells

031 yuanbao basket

032 meal cover

Xu Jianzhang: Around here, there isn't a single steelyard balance not made by me

033 steelyard balance

Yang Qiuling: There is few people are willing to do handicrafts now

034 strainer

035 fly-swatter

Ding Weichang: It takes 80 hours to make a sheet or mat from bamboo stripping

036 bamboo mat

Ms. Pu: Now, the people who wear watches are mostly older people

Zhang Fengxian—Daily wear of elders in Tinglin Town

037 homespun headscarf

038 homespun clothes

039 homespun feeding bib

Wang Genlin: As an apprentice I was unpaid, and I felt honored that my master agreed to teach me

040 rattan chair

Gu Yuexiang—Straw weaving auntie in Xuhang Town

041 straw sandal

Zhou Hongmei: In

order to facilitate more sales, I would go to the countryside with baskets and peddle household by household: "Do you want a basket? "

042 loose weave basket

043 rice basket

Huang Fatang: I used to do it for a living, and now just for fun

044 small bamboo stool

Xu Qiaozhen: On cold days, people come to mend their woolen sweaters, cashmere sweaters and ski jackets

Huang Jinshan—Bamboon weaving Shifu who lives by the river

045 thermos flask with bamboo casing

046 bamboo basket

Gan Lijuan: In the past we earned our living by making straw wares, but today we just do it for fun when we get together

047 straw-plaited Oriental Pearl Tower

048 straw bag

049 straw hat

Zhu Jinlin—A houseware store owner who can make bamboo dragonfly

050 bamboo basket

051 bamboo dragonfly

Yin Yunlian—Runs a variety store by the bus stop

052 copper hand-warmer

Wang Xiuli—I have been selling groceries for 70 years

053 bamboo bian

Shen Yougao: In the past, every household had someone who could do bamboo weaving

054 crab basket

055 strawberry basket

Yu Jinxian: My handmade small baskets are popular even among the foreigners visiting the old town

056 small basket

Tao Qingjian—Iron hammer by the road

057 iron wok

058 iron spoon

059 iron shovel

Mr. Tang: I am probably the youngest among the cotton-fluffing craftsmen

060 cotton quilt padding

Chen Tianxing—Iron

Forger in Xinchang Street

061 funnel

062 water spoon

063 lead bucket

064 youdunzi spoon

065 dustpan

Wang Quanlin: The most popular basket in Jiading is still the yuanbao basket

066 small yuanbao basket

Zha Peihua: All the bicycles I have made are rotatable like the real ones

067 mini tricycle

068 mini bicycle

Mr. Qin: We sell about a thousand items here

Xia Yaoming: You can find the things I made in the stores on Nanjing Road or in Chenghuang Temple

069 mini teapot

070 mini hot water bottle

071 mini hand-warmer

Hua Xuejuan—Weaving auntie in Ping'an Town

072 homespun cotton shoes

Zhu Amei—Forging agricultural tools in Huqiao Town

073 iron rake

Xu Wenhong: Apprentices need to be lessoned, otherwise they would not learn

074 leather slippers

Fei Baoying: I prefer to sell traditional things

075 broom

Wang Xuegen: Every piece of fabric has its own name, I can recognize hundreds of them

Guo Zhigao: I always use the local bamboo from Chongming for the small things I made

076 red-crowned crane

077 bamboo crab

078 small bamboo tray

079 big Chongming basket

Gu Zhenbang—A bamboo ware stall seller in Xianghua Town

080 flail

He Yongdi: The cloth for my wedding was weaved by myself

081 Chongming homespun

082 smart sheep

083 homespun sunhat

084 homespun bag

上海师傅印象

我年幼时四代同堂居住在毗邻南京路的石库门里，自从有记忆开始，目光所及之处，多数都还是手工制品：杯套、碗架、板凳、饭罩、菜篮头……阿太（曾祖母）总是坐在天井的藤椅里，教我怎么称呼过往的每个邻居，楼上楼下来自五湖四海、各行各业的爷叔娘娘伯伯姥姥大妈妈，伴着走廊里无线电的回响说着各自的方言。那时，我所理解的“师傅”，是指那些有手艺的人，他们或步行或推着自行车，走街串巷，补碗盏、修棕绷、卖晾衣裳架子、削刀磨剪刀……人们会随着他们的吆喝声聚拢到一起。等我长高一点了，就跑出弄堂，逛遍了周围的粮油商店、老虎灶、烟纸店，要买什么该去哪里，全都熟记于心。

千禧年后，我家搬离弄堂，住进新的社区。在新家周围的街道晃悠时，我发现这里和 20 世纪 90 年代市中心的街区竟还有些相似，后来才晓得，这里附近的住户基本都是和我们一样，从市区的石库门里弄搬迁过来，所以，原先周边的杂货店也随着他们的老顾客一起迁徙而至。如今，曾经遍布在马路边的杂货店，及那些手作的日用品和师傅们也渐渐地悄然退时，无迹可寻。

嘉定、青浦、奉贤、闵行，上海地区大量的手作日用品曾源自这些地域，给这座大城市带去了环保、简约的日常生活方式。从 2012 年

周祺，1986 年生于上海。上海风景工作室撰稿人、设计师。曾策划“上海篮子”“上海竹编”“父辈的设计”“生活中的上海牌”等城市文化普及展览及活动数十项。著有《上海杂货铺》（同济大学出版社，2013 年）

第一次采访青浦朱家角镇杂货店的朱师傅，到 2019 年年底在嘉定徐行镇碰面的木匠居师傅，在这八年多时间里，受到许许多多的小伙伴、各地的老师以及数不清的路人关照，帮助我在村村户户寻找到一位位行将隐退的手作师傅和那些仍在经营手作日用品的店铺。现在，我将六十余位上海师傅汇集在这本书里，把和他们在一起的时光，以及这座城市最后的手作记忆分享给大家。

周祺

2020 年芒种

Impressions of Shanghai Shifu

When I was young, my family had a house of "four generations under one roof", and lived in a Shikumen next to Nanjing Road. As early as I can recall, handicraft objects were everywhere: cup holders, cupboards, benches, meal covers, shopping baskets… A-Tai (my great grandmother) often sat in a rattan chair on the patio and taught me how to greet each neighbor passing by: Yeshu, Niangniang, Bobo, Laolao, Damama (endearing titles given to men and women of various ages, similar to uncles and aunties). Those living upstairs and downstairs came from all across China and worked in all kinds of jobs, each speaking one's own dialect, mixing with the sound of the radio and drifting along the corridor. At that time, in my understanding, "Shifu" was a term referring to those who are skilled with their hands. They would walk or ride through the streets and alleys, sometimes with their bicycles, fixing a bowl or a zongbeng bed, selling some hangers or sharpening scissors. People would gather around naturally when hearing their peddling sounds. When I grew a little taller, I would run out of the Longtang (a typical Shanghai Lane often with a community built around it) and pop into every shop around the corner: oil and grain shop, old kitchen stove shop, tobacco shop and so on. What to buy where to shop? I knew every shop by heart.

After 2000, our family moved out of the Longtang into a new apartment. To my surprise, I found

Zhou Qi, born in 1986 in Shanghai. Writer and designer for Shanghai View Studio. Curator of various cultural exhibitions and events to promote city heritage, including Shanghai Basket, Shanghai Bamboo Weaving, Designs of the Older Generation, Shanghai Brand in Daily Life, etc. Author of *Shanghai Houswares* (Tongji University Press, 2013)

the new neighborhood quite similar to the old downtown community of the 90s. Later I found out, most of the residents in this quarter are similar to us, gentrified and moved out from Shikumen areas. So the groceries around there also moved, with their old customers, to the new quarter. Now, these sellers who used to be everywhere, have gradually dis appeared and together with them, the handicraft objects and the Shifu.

In Shanghai, most handicrafts for daily use come from these towns and villages in the suburbs of Jiading, Qingpu,Fengxian,Minhang, and bring with them a green and simple lifestyle into the metropolis. Eight years passed from my first interview in 2012, with Zhu Shifu at shop in Zhujiajiao Town, Qingpu District in 2012, to my last interview at the end of 2019, with wooden craftsman Ju Shifu in Xuhang Town, Jiading District. In these 8 years, I came across workshops run by Shifu themselves selling their own crafts, as well as the local shops that are still selling handicrafts for everyday use. I am ever more grateful for the help and support from my friends, teachers and countless strangers. They helped me find one Shifu after another, often close to retirement from village to village. Now, I have collected in this book, 60 handicraft Shifu, sharing with you my memory of them, and the last memory of handicrafts of this city.

Zhou Qi

Grain in Ear (Mangzhong, the 9th Solar Term) 2020

三月的横港
Henggang Village in March

001
常州篮
Changzhou
basket
002
绒线针
knitting
needles

马根发：路上有人开着轿车也会停下来买我东西呢

我到上海快要四十年了，来的时候（还是）一个小伙子。之前我也是打工的，后来公司解散了，就想上海（有什么）买不到的东西，从老家（常熟）带出来卖。现在我一个月回去一次，每次住一个礼拜左右。有时人家东西来不及做，也要等他们做好了再带回上海，有的他们事先就帮我做好了。

原来我只卖毛衣针和衣架，毛衣针挂在身上，衣架就拿在手上。现在织毛衣的人少了，就增加了淘箩、筛子、匾、篮子。脚踏车上的东西都是自己装上去的，每次增加了什么产品，就要考虑放在车子的哪个位置好，现在再多也没有地方好挂了，再加，我车子就不能骑了。

不下雨的话，我早上 5 点起来，把各种产品装到脚踏车上，要花半个小时到一个小时的时间，等装好了再出去。午饭在外面吃，到了一两点回来。下午看情况，有时到 4 点以后再出去一两个小时。顾客 40 ～ 60 岁的多，男的女的都有，路上有人开着轿车也会停下来拦住我买东西呢。我的大部分收入是靠边跑边卖来的，给我一个固定的地方，不一定有生意。

马根发，1954 年生于江苏
2014 年 5 月，虹口区，临平路

Ma Genfa: People stop to buy some stuff from me even when they're driving

It has almost been 40 years since I came to Shanghai. I was a young man at that time. At first, I was working at a company, but later the company was disbanded. So I thought what kind of things could not be found in Shanghai that I could bring from my hometown (Changshu) and sell here. Now, I go back once every month, and stay there for about a week. Sometimes, they are behind the schedule so, I have to wait until the goods are finished, and bring them back to Shanghai. Sometimes, they have already finished in advance.

In the begining, I only sold knitting needles and clothes hangers. I would hang the needles on my body and hold the hangers in my hand. Now, fewer people knit, so I start to sell rice-washing baskets, sieves, bamboo trays, and baskets. I put everything on the bicycle. Every time I add an item to sell, I need to consider where is the best place to display it on the bike. Now there is no room to hang more stuff. If I add more, I will not be able to ride the bike.

If it doesn't rain, I get up at 5 am and put everything on the bike, which takes about half an hour to an hour. After I finish loading, I ride out to sell my wares. Usually I come back around 1 or 2 pm after lunch. Sometimes I go out for an hour or two after 4pm depending on the situation. Most customers are between 40 and 60 years old, both men and women. People would stop to buy some stuff even when they are driving. Most of my income comes from street vending. If you give me a fixed stall, my business may not be good.

Ma Genfa, born in Jiangsu,1954
May. 2014, Linpin Road, Hongkou District

001

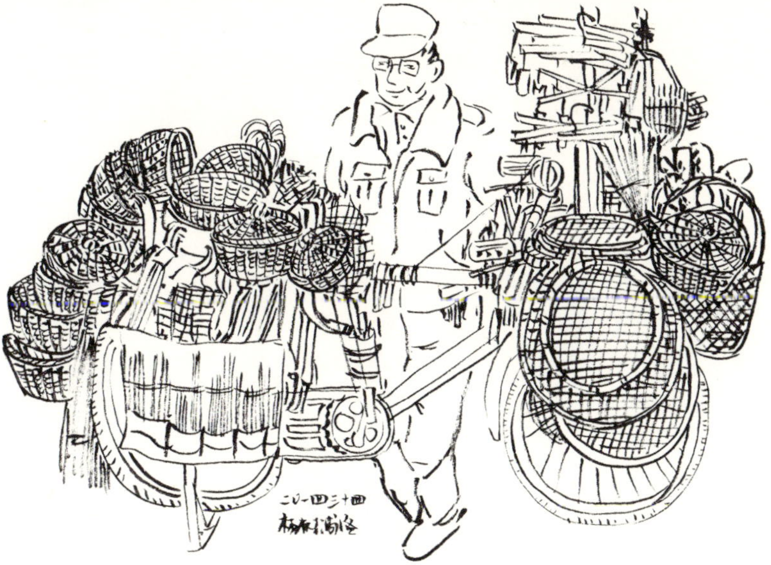

002

003
笪*
da*

*笪：用粗竹篾编成的农具，晒谷物用
* da: bamboo mat used to dry grains

吴德华，1949 年生于上海
2014 年 5 月，浦东新区，虹桥镇

吴德华：竹编这个活儿，只要能想得出来都可以做出来

学这个（竹编）年龄不能超过15岁，不然这个（手）会硬的，手脚不灵活了呀。我10岁学的，手很软，到20岁、30岁没用了，手脚都硬了。

竹编这个活儿，只要能想得出来都可以做出来。这些篮子、笪、匾等等的尺寸都是固定的，就一直是这个大小。我做的这个小笪呢，你拿去洗菜也可以，煮馄饨煮面条往里面一倒（滤水），煮肉出（焯）水也可以用，还有竹子的味道，可以用好几年呢。

这些（竹器）都是用本竹做的，本地的竹子，要去竹行里买，我自己用脚踏车拖回来，一次可以拖6～8根。也没有（劈篾）机器，都是手工劈的，现在这种手艺都被塑料（制品）代替了，也没人肯学了，做这个赚不到钱呀。有次我出去卖（篮子），一个人买了五个，我问他买那么多干嘛（用），他说送人。

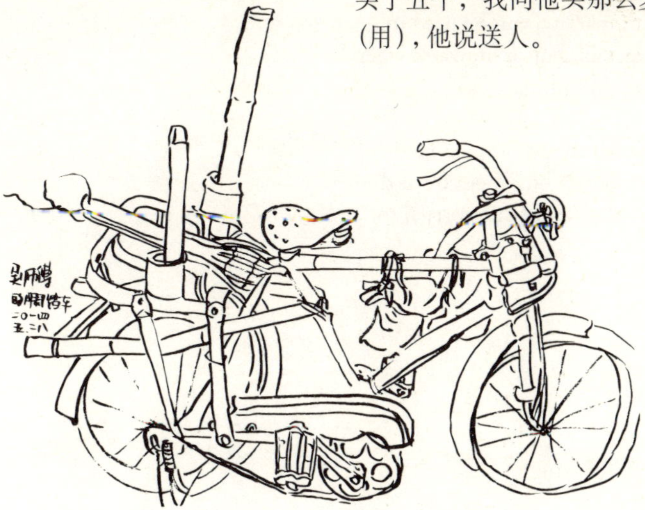

Wu Dehua: For bamboo weaving, you can create anything as long as you have an idea

To learn bamboo weaving, you should be younger than 15 years old. Otherwise your hands get stiff and lose their agility. I learned it when I was 10, and my hands were very soft. When I was 20 or 30 years old, my hands were not so nimble.

For bamboo weaving, you can create anything as long as you have an idea. The sizes of these baskets, da (a rough bamboo mat used to dry grains) and bian (a flat round shallow bamboo basket) are always fixed. For example, this small da that I am making, can be used to wash vegetables or drain water when you cook dumplings.

All these bamboo wares are made of local bamboo. I buy them from the bamboo store and I can carry 6 to 8 bamboos on one trip by bicycle. We have no mie machine (chop the bamboo into thin strips called mie), so we do it by hand. Nowadays, people use plastic products instead of hand-made bamboo wares, and nobody wants to learn this craft, because there's no profit in the trade. I remember once I was selling baskets, and someone bought five. I asked him why he bought so many, and he said he would give them as gifts.

Wu Dehua, born in Shanghai, 1949
May. 2014, Hongqiao Town, Pudong New Area

003

川沙
二〇一四
五廿八

004

升箩*

shengluo*

升箩：用于计量粮食的正方形器皿

shengluo: a measuring apparatus for scooping rice

许文明，1941 年生于上海

2018 年 4 月，崇明区，城桥镇

许文明：退休后就自己做，打发打发时间，就当是玩

这个我们叫升箩，用来量米的，有 3 两 (一个) 的, 7 两的, 1 斤的, 1 斤 6 两的, 2 斤的，一般是用榉木、樟木、水曲柳做的。一个大的大概要做两个钟头：切料、刨料、划线、光料、装配、完刨。早上总归是 8 点钟开始，做到下午三四点。现在还有家里用升箩的，也有人做生日、做寿用来讨口彩（音：升禄）。

做升箩的工具有推刨、钢丝锯、榔头、凿子、大小模具、作凳（工作用的长凳）。现在崇明打（做）农具（工具）的人都没有了，打凿子、斧头。现在店里卖的，跟老早（以前）打出来不一样的，老早打出来的好用。

我是 12 岁开始跟爸爸学的，我爸呢，不讲的，我坐边上看他做呀。真正学是16岁开始。后来(年龄）大起来么就去建筑队做了，还有手工业站、家具厂，在家具厂么做凳子、床、桌子，什么都做的。我是崇明第二家具厂退休的，退休后就自己做，打发打发时间，就当是玩，年纪大了。

Xu Wenming: Since I was retired, I've been doing this to kill time. It's just for fun

We call this shengluo,which is used to measure rice. There is the one for 3 liang (at unit of weight unit; 20 liang equals 1 kilo), 7 liang, 1 jin, (2 jin equals 1 kilo), 1 jin and 6 liang, and 2 jin. Normally, they are made of neem wood, beech wood, camphor wood, or ash wood. It takes about 2 hours to make a big shengluo, involving chopping, planing, marking, polishing, assembling, and finally planing again. Usually, I start working at 8 o'clock in the morning, and finish my work at 3 or 4 pm. Nowadays, there are still some households using shengluo. Some people get shengluo on their birthday for good luck ("shengluo" in Chinese sounds like "get rich").

The tools used to make shengluo include a hand plane, a wire curium, a hammer, a chisel, molds of different sizes, and a work stool. There are few people who forge farming tools, chisels or axes now. The ones sold in the shops are not the same as the hand-forged ones in the old days, which are easier to use.

I started to learn the handicraft from my father at the age of 12. My dad said little, and I just sat next to him and watched him work. When I was 16, I really started getting into it. When I got older, I went to work in the construction crew, and also I worked at the handicraft station and the furniture factory, where I made stools, beds and tables of all sorts. I retired from Chongming No.2 Furniture Factory. Since I was a retired, I've been doing this to kill time. I'm old, and I just do it for fun.

Xu Wenming, born in Shanghai, 1941
Apr. 2018, Chengqiao Town,
Chongming District

004

做升箩
making shengluo

许师傅的工作间
Mr. Xu's workshop

005

铁门

iron gate

俞文归——大团铁艺人

Yu Wengui——An iron craftsman in Datuan Town

005

俞文归，1963 年生于上海
2018 年 3 月，浦东新区，大团镇
Yu Wengui, born in Shanghai, 1963
Mar. 2018, Datuan Town, Pudong New Area

006
竹筐
bamboo
basket

007
竹凳
bamboo
stool

凌旭明：以前我们夏天种地，冬天做篮子

我小时候这里叫凌家宅，川沙县川东乡凌家宅。我 8 岁开始读了三年书，12 岁跟我爸学（竹编），我爸爸妈妈都会的。以前我们夏天种地，冬天做篮子，还养牛，一家人家一只牛，现在地老早不种了呀。

篮有大的、中的、小的，大的（直径）45 公分（厘米），中的是 42 公分，小的是 36 公分。有盖子的篮是盛饭用的。我们做好么有人来批（进货）的呀，那时买的人多得不得了。有一段时候个人不能做的，属于“小农经济”，走资本主义道路。最最苦的时候，拿个篮去问供销社做山芋（番薯）的换山芋干吃。

蒸笼我也做的，没师傅教，我自己拿蒸笼拆开来看看（就会了）。做竹椅子也没师傅教的，做一个大约要半天，竹子烧到 65（摄氏）度，再弯，不能烧太久，烧得不好要断掉的。这个椅子靠背比较高，方便岁数大的人头可以靠着。做椅子的竹子，大多数都是冬天砍下来的，长满五年的竹子最好，太嫩么要蛀掉的。

凌旭明，1934 年生于上海
2017 年 3 月，浦东新区，大团镇

Ling Xuming: In the old days, we would farm in summer and make baskets in winter

When I was young, this place here was still called Lingjia Zhai (the house of Family Ling; also the village name), which is located in Chuandong County, Chuansha District. I went to school when I was 8 years old and studied for 3 years. At the age of 12, I started to learn bamboo weaving with my father, because my parents both knew the craft. In the old days, we farmed in summer and made baskets in winter, and we also raised cattle. Every household had cattle. Now, we don't farm anymore.

There are different sizes of baskets, including big, medium and small. The big one is 46 centimeters (diameter), the medium one is 42 centimeters, and the small one is 36 centimeters. The baskets with lids are used to serve rice. People would come to buy our baskets once they were finished. In the old times, our business was very good. But there was a time that individual business was not allowed , because it was considered to be "capitalist". During the most difficult time, we would go to the Trading Co-op and exchange a basket for a sweet potato at the potato stall.

I can also make steamers. No one taught me and I just dissembled a steamer and examined its structure. Neither was there a shifu to teach me how to make bamboo chairs. It takes about half a day to make a chair. You need to heat the bamboo to 65 degrees then bend it. You can't heat it for too long, otherwise it will be broken. This chair has a long back, for older people so they can rest their heads on it. The bamboo used to make chairs is mostly cut in winter. The best ones are those that have fully grown for 5 years and the tender ones are easily eaten by worms.

Ling Xuming, born in Shanghai, 1934
Mar. 2017, Datuan Town, Pudong New Area

工具
tools

凌师傅的工作间
Mr. Ling's workshop

006

007

008
金鱼灯
goldfish
lantern

李政：天上飞的，地上跑的，只要画得出图纸我就能做出来

我从小喜欢画画，没有正式拜过老师，都是自己买点书看看画画，小学三四年级就开始出黑板报、刻蜡纸了。我也喜欢手工，做航模、船模什么的。后来在丝织厂里搞宣传和文体工作，布置宣传橱窗，介绍劳模、先进。(20 世纪) 80 年代末，我还给黄浦旅游节做过几次龙车、彩车。

老早（以前）只要江浙一带哪里有灯会，我都会去看的，南京、苏州，还有海盐，我蛮喜欢扬州的彩灯。从厂里调到文化宫里上班后，我就刻写蜡纸油印了教材，辅导基层爱好者，到过颛桥、曹路文化站去指导。以前我们是住杨浦区的，现在动迁了，住到新场后开了这家李氏灯彩铺。退休了没事情，弄着玩。

天上飞的，地上跑的，只要你画得出图纸我就能做出来。金鱼灯一般都是大红的、粉红的，我做了有三十年了，一天顶多做三只，多了也做不出的。做灯最关键的是骨架要做好。宫灯更加难做点，宫灯复杂，需要时间长，上面的装饰多呀，上面的花样要弄很长时间。

李政，1951 年生于上海
2019 年 3 月，浦东新区，新场镇，
洪东街 17 号，李氏灯彩铺

Li Zheng: Whether the creature is flying in the sky or running on the ground, I can make it if you can draw the sketch

I have been very fond of drawing since I was a kid. I learned drawing through self-study instead of teachers' instruction. From Grade 3 and 4 in the primary school, I started to create artworks on the blackboards at school. I also liked handicrafts, such as making model ships or airplanes. Later, I worked for publicity in a silk factory. I was in charge of making the publicity boards, introducing model workers. In the late 1980s, I made dragon chariots and parade floats used in the Huangpu Tourist Festival for a couple of times.

In the past, I would visit any lantern festivals if they were held in Zhejiang or Jiangsu province. I have been to the festival in Nanjing, Suzhou and Haiyan, and I quite like the colorful lanterns of Yangzhou. Later, my job was transferred from the factory to a cultural hall, and then I published some handbooks of stencil making. I have also mentored local cultural works in the Zhuanqiao and Caolu town, and tutored some local art enthusiasts. I used to live in Yangpu District, but after my relocation, I moved to Xinchang and opened this lantern shop. I'm retired and have nothing to do, so I open this shop for fun.

Whether the creature is flying in the sky or running on the ground, I can make it if you can draw the sketcn. I have been doing this for 30 years and I can make up to 3 lanterns a day. The key of lantern-making is to make a good structure. "Palace lanterns" are more difficult to make. Because of the complicated structures, decorations and patterns, they take longer hours to make them.

Li Zheng, born in Shanghai, 1951
Mar. 2019, Li's Color Lantern Shop, No. 17, Hongdong Street, Xinchang Street, Pudong New Area

做金鱼灯
making goldfish lantern

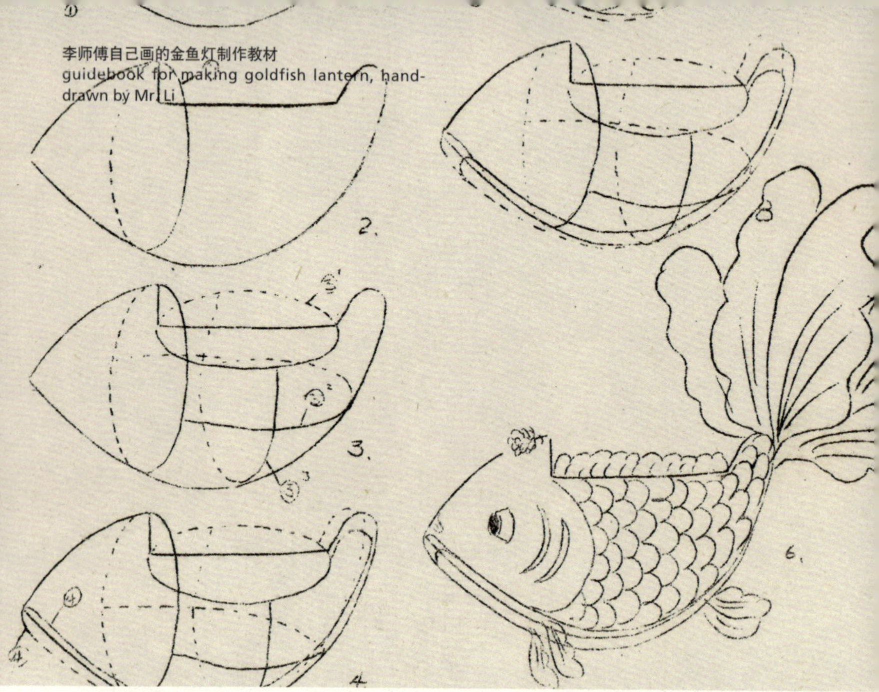

李师傅自己画的金鱼灯制作教材
guidebook for making goldfish lantern, hand-drawn by Mr. Li

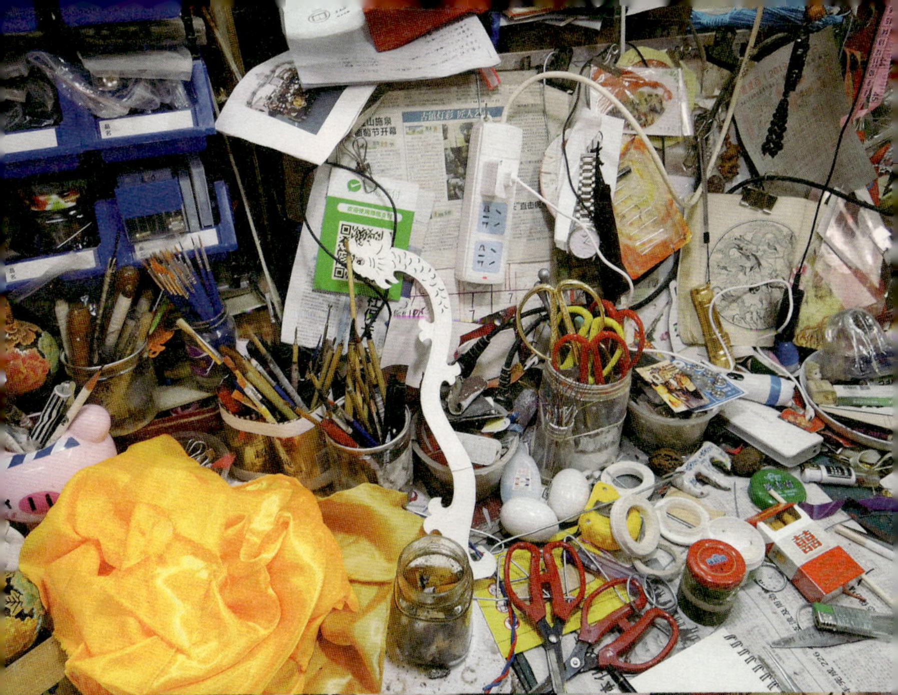

李师傅的工作间
Mr. Li's workshop

009
筅帚*
xianzhou*
010
蒸架
steaming
lattice
011
百脚架*
hundred-arm
hanger*
衣架.
脚架
洗帚.
蒸格.
蝇拍.

薛文华：再过十年这种竹编的东西真的没有人做了

川沙老早（以前）就有柴场村和大洪墩这两个地方专门做竹器的，我这里卖的四角篮、六角篮都是当地的特色。最早的时候篮子只有几角钱一个，家家户户都有的呀。再过十年这种竹编的东西真的没有人做了，我们当地做的师傅都70岁左右了，到老了就做不动了。

我这家店没名字，自己开的嘛，就叫竹器店。店是1982年我父母开的，后来他们岁数大了，80多岁做不动了，就叫我来了。我小时候是学木工的，我祖父和父亲以前也都是木工，后来我父母他们一个朋友圈子里很多人做竹编，他们也就学起来了，那时候是跟师傅学的。会竹编的女的好像以前就我母亲一个人，大多数是男的。

我这里有三十来个品种，卖的最好的么就是蒸笼，私人饭店用得多。我也会做点小东西，百脚架（折叠晾衣架）、吊升（舀酒的器具），还有蒸菜用的饭架，带脚的么放在平底锅里用，不带脚的么放在炒菜锅里用，还有大的小的筅帚。筷笼要人家定了再做，没定的做好放着时间长了干掉就不好用了。现在竹器这个东西买的人少了，都被塑料啊不锈钢啊代替掉了。

* 筅帚：刷锅子用的竹刷子
* xianzhou: pot-scouring brush made of bamboo
* 百脚架：撑开如百脚（蜈蚣）一般，有很多夹子的晾衣架
* hundred-arm hanger: a hanger with many clips, looks like a centipede when open

薛文华，1964年生于上海
2019年4月，浦东新区，川沙镇，操场街15号

Xue Wenhua: In another 10 years, there will be no one for bamboon craft.

In Chuansha Town, there are two places that specialized in making bamboo wares, Chaichang Village and Dahong Village. What I sell here-square baskets and hexagon baskets-are local specialties. In the old days, every household had one basket which cost a few pennies. In another 10 years, there will be really no one who can make these kinds of bamboo wares. Our local shifu (masters) are about 70 years old. They won't be able to do it anymore when they get older.

My shop has no name and it is simply called the Bamboo ware Shop. It was opened in 1982 by my parents. Whey they grew old, they couldn't manage it anymore in their eighties, so they asked me to run it. Originally, I was an apprentice of carpentry, since both my grandfather and father were carpenters. Later, many friends of my parents started to do bamboo wares, so they started to learn bamboo weaving under the instruction of a shifu. My mother was perhaps the only female among the bamboo-weavers, most of whom were men.

I have about 30 kinds of products to sell here. The bestseller is the steamers, as many private restaurants use them. I can also make some bric-a-bracs, like folded hangers, diaosheng (a tool to measure wine, which has a lucky tune), steaming shelves (to heat up dishes)-the ones with legs are used in flat pans and the ones without areis used in wok pots-and brooms. Chopstick holders are only made by orders, because they will get dry and go bad if you premake them without any order and left them there for too long. Nowadays, bamboo-wares are no long popular and they've been replaced by plastic and steel alternatives.

Xue Wenhua, born in Shanghai, 1964
Apr. 2019, No.15, Caochang Street,
Chuansha Town, Pudong New Area

009
010
純天然竹夹

011

012
篮
basket

蔡英龙——在庄行镇上卖杂货

Cai Yinglong——General store peddler in Zhuanghang Town

012

蔡英龙，1962 年生于上海
2019 年 3 月，奉贤区，庄行镇，
庄行东街 8 号
Cai Yinglong, born in Shanghai, 1962
Mar. 2019, No. 8, East Zhuanghang Street,
Zhuanghang Town, Fengxian District

013
蚌壳棉鞋*
shell-shaped cotton shoes*

014
圆口鞋
round-mouth shoes

015
搭襻鞋
strap shoes

*蚌壳棉鞋：如蚌壳形状的棉鞋
*shell-shaped cotton shoes: cotton shoes in shell shape

杨慎喜：不管什么鞋子，我只要一看就会做

我们店在新中国成立前就叫杨瑞记了。我爸爸是“小花园”（上海老字号布鞋店）出来的，他们的小圆口鞋子最有名了。11岁的时候，我白天读书，晚上学生意。我这双鞋子是庄行（镇）的特产，老早（以前）这边有四家鞋铺，1958年的时候并拢到一起，我是负责人。1983年解散了，我继续开店。

做鞋子总共有十七道工序。先要划样子，剪出来，然后开始扎鞋底，鞋底用十四层全棉的布。扎好底做衬底，再做鞋面。做鞋面的时候拷边蛮难的，要缝得整整齐齐。然后绱鞋子——用上了蜜蜡的棉线，把鞋底、衬底和鞋面缝起来。用楦头撑鞋子是最后的步骤，撑好后洗一下拿出去晒干。

不管什么鞋子我只要一看就会做，最小大概12码，大的做到44码。老早没有套鞋的时候，我们还做一种落雨天穿的钉鞋，在面子上涂上桐油防水。在布鞋上面缝两个绒线做的绒球，这样就是结婚时候穿的鞋子。冬天做棉鞋多，老早来买的都是本地老顾客，现在也有从市区特地找过来的。我今年80多岁，再做一年也不做了，年纪大了做不动了。

杨慎喜，1937年生于上海
2019年3月，奉贤区，庄行镇，
庄行东街26号，杨瑞记鞋铺

Yang Shenxi: No matter what kinds of shoes they are, I only need to have a look and I can make them

Our store was always called Yang Rui Ji even before liberation. My father used to work for the Brand - "Little Garden" (a time-honored Shanghai brand for traditional cloth shoes), which was most famous for its small round-collar shoes. At the age of 11, I was going to school in the daytime and learning the business at night. This pair of shoes I am wearing is a special product of Zhuanghang Town. In the old days, there were 4 shoe shops here . In 1958, they merged into a handcraft trading cooperative operation, and I was in charge of the group. In 1983, the co-op was disbanded, and I continued to run my own shop.

There are 17 steps to make a pair of shoes. First, you draw the shape and cut it out. Then you start to bind the bottom sole, which is made of 14 layers of cotton. After finishing the sole, you make the insole and then the vamp. The edge of seaming is quite difficult when you make the vamp, because it needs to be very neat. After that, you stitch the sole, the insole and the vamp together with waxed cotton threads. Finally, you use a shoe last to stretch the shoe into shape, and then wash and dry it.

No matter what kinds of shoes they are I only need to have a look and I can make them. The smallest size I have made is only 12 (Eur), and the biggest is 44 (Eur). In the old days, without overboots, we made a kind of spike shoe with the vamp covered with waterproof oil especially for rainy days. The cloth shoes with two crochet wool balls on top are specially made for weddings. In winter, we make cotton-padded shoes. In the past, most customers were local people. Now, more and more customers are coming from the city center. I am over 80 years old and can only keep the store running for one more year and then close my business. I can't shoulder the workload any more owing to my old age.

Yang Shenxi, born in Shanghai, 1937
Mar. 2019, Yang Rui Ji Shoe Shop,
No.26, East Zhuanghang Street,
Zhuanghang Town, Fengxian District

013
014
015

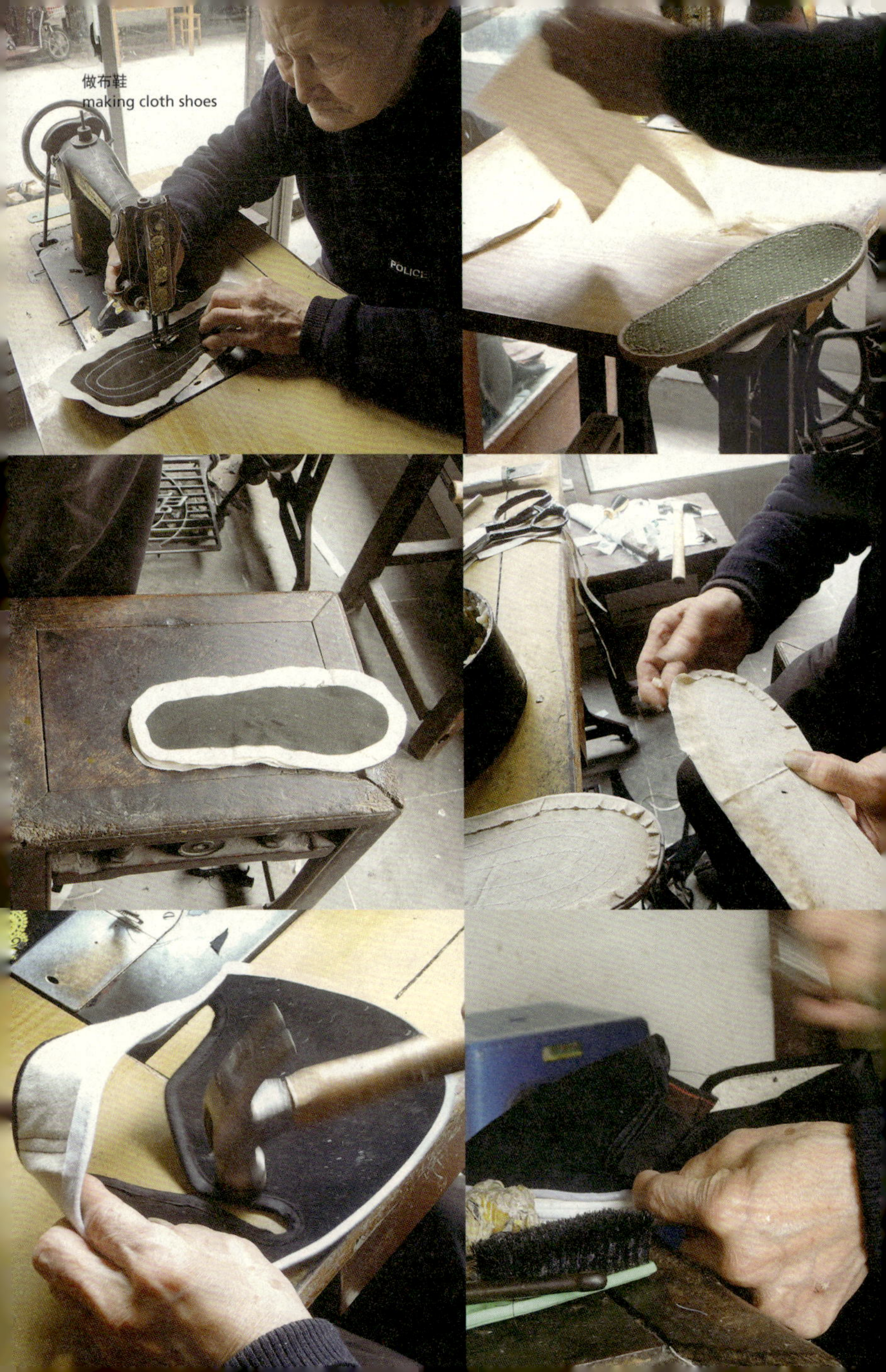

做布鞋
making cloth shoes

016
蒲鞋*
rush shoes*

017
草鞋
straw shoes

*蒲鞋：用芦苇或稻草编制的鞋子，冬天保暖
* rush shoes: shoes made of weeds or straws, very warm for winters

庄金生：现在蒲鞋只能看看了

我 12 岁时地里（的活）已经样样会做了，大概 15 岁时摊（做）蒲鞋，一开始我父母做草鞋、蒲鞋的时候，我在旁边看看。碰到落雨地里做不了啥，各么（那）就摊双蒲鞋，自己做了自己穿。街上也有人做了出来卖的，改革开放之后蒲鞋比较少了，钞票么多了，买双鞋子就好了吧，保暖鞋呀，现在大家穿的这种。

芦苇是出去寻（找）的呀，九十月份，每天（骑）脚踏车出去，看见么就后面一绑，现在很难寻了，搞卫生用药水打光了。芦秆么造房子好用的，芦叶么包粽子，芦花可以做扫帚、蒲鞋。芦苇采回来呢不能摆在太阳里晒，要放在家里阴干，十几天，不然要霉掉的，烦得很呢。

摊蒲鞋第一步就是搓稻草绳子做（鞋）底呀，底完成之后，把毛茸茸的芦花编上去，就是做蒲鞋的面，摊面，摊好么拿布头用针线把鞋口滚好么就好了呀。蒲鞋不分左右脚的。老早（以前）农村都是烂泥地，冬天适合穿蒲鞋，现在都是水泥地了，蒲鞋要磨坏的。现在，蒲鞋只能看看了。

庄金生，1933 年生于上海
2019 年 3 月，浦东新区，泥城镇

做蒲鞋
making rush shoes

Zhuang Jinsheng: Nowadays, rush shoes are only for exhibition

At the age of 12, I was qualified for all kinds of work in the field. Around 15 years old, I started to make rush shoes. At first, I stood by and watched them when my parents were making straw shoes or rush shoes. When it came to rainy days and there wasn't much to do in the field, I'd make a pair of rush shoes for myself. There were also people selling their home-made rush shoes. But after the reform and opening, rush shoes became rare. Now, people are better off, they can afford any good shoes like the ones that keep them warm.

You need to look for rushes in the wild. In September or October, I'll ride a bike out and I'll put rushes on the bike if I have found some. It's difficult to find them now, though. To keep the fields clean, some herbicides are used and have killed all rushes. The stalks can be used to build houses, the weed leaves can be used to wrap zongzi and the flowers can be used to make brooms and rush shoes. The freshly-picked rushes cannot be dried under the sun, but they have to be dried in the shade for 12 days. If you don't do this, rushes can get mouldy, which is very troublesome.

To make rush shoes, first you need to break the straws and make a sole. Then you weave the fluffy weed flowers onto it with the vamp formed. Finally, you use cloth and a needle to bind the collar. There is no left and right for rush shoes. In the old days, the country roads were full of mud, people wore rush shoes in winter. Now, there are all concrete roads, and rush shoes are easily worn out. Now, rush shoes are only for exhibition.

Zhuang Jinsheng, born in Shanghai, 1933
Mar. 2019, Nicheng Town, Pudong New Area

庄师傅的工作间
Mr. Zhuang's workshop

018

小兔子灯*

small rabbit lantern*

*兔子灯：元宵节时儿童玩的兔子形状的纸花灯

* rabbit lantern: a paper lantern in the shape of rabbit for children at Lantern Festival

王宏春——老师傅和小兔子灯

Wang Hongchun ——The old Shifu and the small rabbit lantern

王宏春，1942 年生于上海
2013 年 4 月，浦东新区，浦三路
Wang Hongchun, born in Shanghai, 1942
Apr. 2013, Pusan Road, Pudong New Area

019

节约领*

detachable callar*

*节约领：为节约衣料制成的假领子

*detachable callar: a detachable collar made to save cloth

张乐华：全世界只要有华人的地方，就会有假领子市场

我们这家店是20世纪50年代公私合营的时候开的，最早叫“静安区百货修配商店”，都是住在静安区的小商小贩集中到一起，做点修修补补（的工作）。现在修家用电器、衣服改大小、补羊毛衫和修棉毛衫裤也都还有。老早（以前）王双庆（已故上海著名滑稽艺术家）来接裤脚管，他买的棉毛裤，洗两次缩短了么就拿过来接接长。

我们这里卖一些老百姓平常用得到的东西，从2块起。百雀羚、海鸥洗头膏、永芳珍珠膏、蛤蜊油、头油、甘油、染发用的披肩、手帕、洗热水瓶的水垢去除剂、缝纫机油等等。卖得最好的是假领子，也叫节约领，我们的花色、尺寸比较多。全世界只要有华人的地方，就会有假领子市场，保安、差头司机和一些怀旧的人特别喜欢。

很多顾客都以为北京百货商店很大的，没想到跑过来一看是家不起眼的小店。他们讲，其他市场上买不到的东西，如果你们北京百货商店也买不到么就总归买不到了，说明对我们店相当期待。不过这里可能要面临拆迁，我们正在寻找可以合作的新门面，把这家老商店保留下来。

张乐华，1958年生于上海
2015年4月，静安区，石门二路156号，北京百货店

Zhang Lehua: Wherever there are Chinese people, there will be a market for detachable collars

Our shop was opened in 1950, when public-private partnerships were introduced. In the beginning, it was called "Jing'an Department Store for Repairs and Supply Replacements", where peddlers living in Jing'an District gathered together and made some tinkering business. Today, there are still some people repairing household appliances, tailoring clothes, mending holes on woolen sweaters and altering cotton underwear. A long time ago, Wang Shuangqing (a popular but late comedian based in Shanghai) came to lengthen his trouser legs, because his cotton trousers shrank after having been a washed a few times.

We sell daily supplies here which common people can afford like Pechoin skin-care products, Seagull shampoos, Yongfang pearl creams, clam oils, hair oils, glycerins, shawls and handkerchiefs for hair coloring, descalers for cleansing hot water bottles, sewing-machine oils and so on with some products cost as low as 2 yuan. The bestseller is the detachable collar, also called the economic collar. We sell various designs and sizes of detachable collar. Wherever there are Chinese people, there will alway be a market for detachable collars. Security guards, taxi drivers and nostalgic people love them very much.

Many customers think the Beijing Department Store would be a very big store before they get here. To their surprise, it is only a small shop when they saw it with their own eyes. There is a saying, when you want to buy something that you can't find it in the market, please go to the Beijing Department Store and have a look.You can't find it anywhere else if you can't find it in our store. It means that they have very high expectations for us. But it is said that this area will be demolished and gentrified soon.We are looking for a new place to collaborate with, so that we can keep this old store running.

Zhang Lehua, born in Shanghai, 1958
Apr. 2015, Beijing Department Store,
No. 156, Shimen No.2 Road, Jing'an District

020
蒸糕桶
cake barrels

020

徐冬林：我带过二十七个徒弟

我17岁的时候在家里学的生意，过去学生意都是学三年帮三年，总共六年。师傅就像皇帝一样的，什么事情都要帮他准备好，早上起来，要把水打好给他洗脸，早饭烧好，晚上洗脚，家里什么活都要做的，要做三年呢。三年学好了还要帮三年，再要学学好。我们老早（以前）一个村庄都是做这个东西（圆作）的。大概25岁的时候，我就跟师傅到上海。

蒸糕桶要用老的杉木做，江西的最好。经过选料、锯料、钻眼、镶竹钉、组合、刨、箍，按照老法来做的话，不用胶水，全部用竹钉来组合。一般每次不会只做一个的，十个十个一做，(这样）做得快呀。工具有圆刨、平刨、角刨、里刨、底刨、直刨、手擦钻、角尺、圆尺、锯子、多角刀、斜刀、斜凿。

我自己后来也带过二十七个徒弟，最多的时候我们有十几个人在一起工作，昆山（江苏省）、周庄（江苏省）、乌镇（浙江省）都去做过。冬天是我们的旺季，经常有人来定做的。

徐冬林，1945年生于江苏
2018年4月，闵行区，七宝镇，北横沥路44号

做蒸糕桶
making cake barrels

Xu Donglin: I used to have 27 apprentices

I learnt the business at home when I was 17 years old. In the old days, it took 6 years to learn a business, which included 3 years' learning and 3 years' assistance. Shifu (the master) was like an emperor. You needed to prepare everything for him. In the morning, you'd prepare the water for him to wash his face and cook breakfast and in the evening, you'd wash his feet, and do the rest of the chores in the house, which lasted three years! Then you would assist the master for three more years after having learned the craft. It's important to consolidate your skills. In the past, my whole village did this business. When I was about 25 years old, I came to Shanghai with my shifu.

When making rice-steaming barrels, you need old Chinese fir woods, of which the best comes from Jiangxi Province. The making procedure is as follows: select materials, saw them, drill holes, inlay bamboo nails, assemble, trim, and hoop the barrel. Following the traditional method, we don't use glues at all; the whole barrel is assembled with bamboo nails. Usually, we don't make only one barrel once and it would be more efficient to make 10 for every batch. The tools included circular plane, flat plane, angle plane, inside plane, bottom plane, straight plane, hand drill, angle ruler, circular ruler, saw, multi-angle knife, skew knife, and skew chisel.

I used to have 27 apprentices. When the business was good, we had more than 10 people working together, and we went to work in Kunshan (in Jiangsu Province), Zhou Zhuang (also in Jiangsu) and Wuzhen (in Zhejiang Province). Winter is high season, and many people come here for their custom-made orders.

Xu Donglin, born in Jiangsu, 1945
Apr. 2018, No. 44, Noth Hengli Road, Qibao Town, Minhang District

021
笼格
bamboo
steamers

魏鹏飞——最年长的竹编师傅
Wei Pengfei——The eldest bamboo weaving Shifu

魏鹏飞，1922 年生于上海
2014 年 5 月，虹口区，海伦路 371 号，顺昌蒸笼店（歇业）
Wei Pengfei, born in Shanghai, 1922
May. 2014, Shunchang Bamboo Steamer Shop, No.371 Hailun Road, Hongkou District (closed)

022
提篮
hand-held basket

023
竹帽
bamboo hat

024
竹衣架
bamboo hanger

025
竹夹
bamboo clip*

顺兴春竹器

*竹夹：餐饮业用于夹取食物的用具
bamboo clip: a tool used to pick up food in the food industry

顾玲娣：以前这里有篾竹街*，所有的店都是卖竹器的

顺兴泰这个抬头是老祖宗传下来的，有一百多年了。我老爹（爷爷）传给我爸，我爸传给我哥哥，然后我哥哥再传到我。我过个两年做不动了，就传给我儿子。

我老爹以前都是自己做自己卖，还带徒弟。我爸手艺好，会做的东西多了。(20 世纪）50 年代后店铺合并进厂，我爸在上海有名的百花竹器厂上班，里面有几百个工人，专门编匾的编匾，专门编篮子的编篮子，产品有几百种几千种东西。

过去我们也请师傅来家里做，跟我们住一起吃一起，大到笼格（蒸笼)，小到挖耳朵的什么都做，有时候还帮我们做点自己用的小东西，我们吃饭用的筷子也是他做的。有的师傅自己也会兜上来（找生意）的，会问你要做什么，可以帮你做。像做篮子、淘（米）箩是浙江的，做竹椅、笼屜（蒸笼）是安徽的，都是有固定的师傅来帮我们做的。

店里主要是靠老客户订货，没有订单没办法生存的。以前这里有篾竹街，所有的店都是卖竹器的，有二三十家，现在就剩下我们一两家了。

顾玲娣，1952 年生于上海
2019 年 3 月，黄浦区，中华路 308 号，顺兴泰竹器店

* 篾竹街：上海老城厢东门外专营竹器商品的街区，早期称篾竹弄，已有百年历史

Gu Lingdi: This used to be the street for mie bamboo and every shop sold bamboo wares

The shop's name "Shun Xing Tai" is inherited from my old generations and it has existed for over 100 years. My father inherited it from my grandfather, then my father passed it on to my brother and at present I own the shop. My son will inherit it in two years, when I am too old too run it.

My grandfather did everything himself. He sold the stuff he made and trained apprentices. My father also had good craft skills and could do many craftwork. In the 1950s, our shop was merged into a larger factory, and so my father worked for the famous Bai Hua Bamboo Wares Factory in Shanghai. There were hundreds of workers making thousands of different products, some of them making bian, a flat round split-bamboo basket, some doing regular baskets.

In the past, we also invited a shifu to our house, who would eat and live with us. He could make everything-big wares like steamers, or small ones like ear picks, as well as some small daily wares, like chopsticks. Some Shifu would come up to you to ask what you want. Shifu who are from Zhejiang generally make baskets and rice-washing baskets, while bamboo chairs and steamers are made mostly by Anhui shifu, who are all specialists.

Now, the shop mainly depends on our regular customers. Our shop can't be run without their orders. It used to be the street for mie bamboo, where all the shops (about 20-30) sold bamboo wares. Now there is only one or two shops left, including us.

* Mie Bamboo Street was also known as Mie Bamboo Lane in the early days. It was a neighborhood outside the East Gate of Shanghai Old Town where numerous bamboo ware shops were grouped together. It has a history of over 100 years

Gu Lingdi, born in Shanghai, 1952
Mar. 2019, Shun Xing Tai Bamboo Ware Shop, No.308, Zhonghua Road, Huangpu District

顾阿姨的丈夫沈师傅在顺兴泰竹器店内
Mr.Shen (husband of Ms.Gu) in Shun Xing Tai Bamboo Ware Shop

023

024
025

Baxiao Village in June

026
腰圆包
straw bag

027
草帽
straw hat

028
草拖鞋
straw slippers

029
杯套
cup holder

030
糖果盒
candy box
basket

026

孙逸娟，1949 年生于上海
2013 年 8 月，嘉定区，东大街 314 号
秋霞圃，三隐堂

孙逸娟：(20 世纪）70 年代的时候出口订单最多

草编我 9 岁的时候就学了，读书的时候，妈妈做么，就跟着一起做，一般都是大人做，小孩跟着做的呀。我女儿也是的呀，我做么她看着，帮帮忙，帮你小弄弄（简单的活），那么就继承了，就一直做了。

(20 世纪）70 年代的时候订单最多，一开始是做拖鞋，后来么做杯垫、做包，很多都是广交会出口的，国家来收（购）的。有时候来不及做么就夜里做通宵，家里一只油灯，然后几个人围拢起来，一边做一边听广播，里面放样板戏，大家还跟着一起唱唱，也蛮闹忙（热闹）的。夜里我们做了晚了，我妈就烧咸酸饭（菜饭）给我们吃。一个礼拜（一周）卖掉一些么平时好零用用（当零花钱）。

黄草是自己种的。种草很辛苦，3 月份松土、落籽（播种）。一个半月后要落苗、插秧，像种水稻一样。那么到大伏天开始拔草，要收了。草编热天、冷天呢都不好，太干了。最好是落雨天，要有点湿度，黄梅天编正正好好。

Sun Yijuan: In the 1970s, we got a lot of export orders

I started to learn straw weaving at the age of 9 when I was still in school. I helped my mom weave when she was doing it. It was very common that the kids watched and learned from elders. My daughter learnt it from me, who started to make some simple stuffs. And gradually, she acquired the skills and kept doing it.

We got the most orders in the 1970s. At first, we made slippers, and then coasters and bags. Most of these orders were for exports traded at the Canton Fairs (China Import and Export Fair in Guangzhou), and they were from the government. Sometimes, we didn't have enough time to make them all, so we had to stay up all night. With an oil lamp burning, we gathered and worked together while listening to the radio. The radio was playing Yangbanxi (Cultural Revolution operas) and we would sing along. It was a quite lively scene. At night, if we stayed up late, mom would cook vegetable rice with salted meat for us. Every week, we sold a batch of finished products and got some pocket money.

We planted the yellow grass by ourselves, which was a hard job. In March, you loosed the soil and sowed the seeds. Then one month and a half later, you planted the seedlings, like planting rice. At the hottest time of the summer, we pulled out the weeds and got ready for reaping.

If the weather was too hot or too cold, it was not suitable for straw weaving because of the drought. The best time was the rainy days, when it was wet. Huangmei (the rainy season) is a perfect period for weaving.

Sun Yijuan, born in Shanghai , 1949
Aug. 2013, San Ying Tang, Qiuxiapu Garden, No. 314 Dongda Street, Jiading District

027

028

029

030

牡丹图案腰圆包
straw bag with peony pattern

031
元宝篮
yuanbao basket

032
饭罩*
meal cover*

赵士德，1935 生于上海
2013 年 6 月，嘉定区，徐行镇
Zhao Shide, born in Shanghai, 1935
Jun. 2013, Xuhang Town, Jiading District

*饭罩，用于遮罩饭菜的罩子
* meal cover: used to cover dishes

赵士德——边做边卖的竹匠

Zhao Shide——Bamboo artisan who both makes and sells

031

032

033
秤杆
steelyard
balance

徐建章：小菜场里没有一根不是我的秤

大团镇都知道我的，小菜场里没有一根不是我的秤。以前来买秤都要一个礼拜后才能拿到，我都来不及做。这两天是淡季，到了夏收、秋收就要忙了。

小的时候在家里看着爸爸做，爸爸是拜师傅学的，新中国成立前开自己的秤店，公私合营之后么就进单位了。那个时候（20世纪）60年代，我初中毕业，正好有规定员工可以带一个子女进单位，我就去学了三年。

以前么秤杆都是用老红木做的，现在用桐糙(一种硬木的名称)。人工大呀（费时)，木头买来，刨圆，然后用水磨，上颜色，再水磨，嵌秤星(秤杆上的计量刻度)，最后还要磨磨光，总共要五六道工序。嵌秤星老早（以前）都是用银子的，现在用铝合金了。以前秤杆上面还有人画图写字，仙鹤啊、龙啊、蛇啊，秤口上也可以雕刻出花样，雕好后也用银子嵌进去，现在做这种秤的人没了。

家里小孩老早喊我不要做了，我呢没有别的兴趣爱好，就做秤。我今年实足70岁，现在眼睛不行了，生意也没以前好了，就准备做到明年年底结束。现在么都用电子秤了，这个是时代发展，你可惜也没办法呀。

徐建章，1956年生于上海
2014年6月，浦东新区，大团镇，
永春东路38号，众鑫秤店

Xu Jianzhang: Around here, there isn't a single steelyard balance not madc by me

I am quite famous in Datuan Town. Around here, there isn't a single steelyard balance (a traditional type of scales) not made by me. In the past, you would need to wait for a week if you came to buy steelyard balances, because I had many orders. It is off-season now. I will get busy when it comes to harvest seasons in summer and autumn.

When I was a kid, I watched my father make steelyard balances, who learnt the craft from a master. Before the liberation, my father was running his own balance shop. Later he became an employee of the company after the joint state-private ownership system was introduced. In the 1960s, I had just graduated from a junior middle school. At that time, the company had a policy that every employee could take one of their children to join in, so I went to study for 3 years.

It requires a lot of labor to make balance. We buy the wood, plane it, polish it, then color it and polish it again, we carve the graduated scales (chengxing, literally meaning balance stars); finally, we polish and shine it. Originally, the scales was made by silver but now wc use aluminum alloy as an alternative. In the past, people would also draw or do calligraphy on the arms, like cranes, dragons or snakes; and the tips were also carved into various shapes and patterns, then embedded with silver. Nowadays, there is no one who is willing to make this kind of steelyard balance.

My kids asked me to stop the business, but I have no hobbies except making these balances. I am 70 years old now with poor eye sight. The business is not as good as it was in the old days. So I am planning to close it by the end of next year. It is the era of technological innovation, and people prefer to use electric balances. There is no turning back even if you think it is a pity.

工具
tools

Xu Jianzhang, born in Shanghai, 1956
Jun. 2014, Zhongxin Steelyard Shop, No. 38, East Yongchun Road, Datuan Town, Pudong New Area

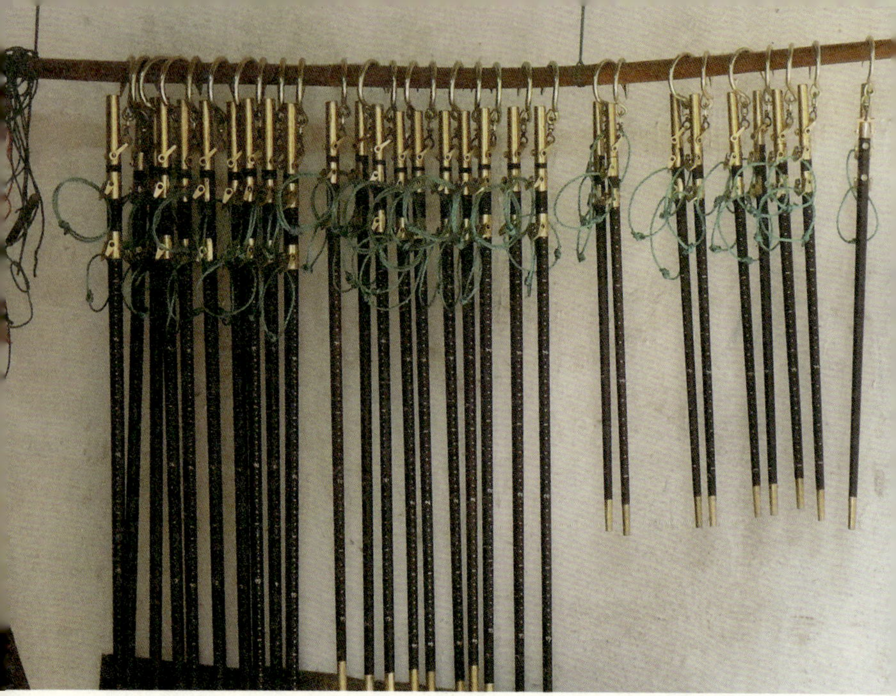

二〇一四二六

做秤杆
making steelyard balance

034
笊篱*
strainer*

035
苍蝇拍
fly-swatter

*笊篱：用于捞东西，能漏水的炊具
*strainer: kitchenware for straining water and taking out cooked food

*篾竹村：源于明末清初以编织竹器为营的村落，位于嘉定城南，现为马陆镇众芳村

杨秋玲，1955 年生于上海
2013 年 8 月，嘉定区，嘉定镇

杨秋玲：手工的东西很少人肯做了

圆篮、四角篮、糠筛、米筛、箩……每种东西都会卖完的，手工的东西很少人肯做了。州桥以前卖竹编的店大概有五六家，现在只剩我一个了。这个摊以前是我婆婆在摆的，二十年前她过世后，我就从厂里面辞职，过来摆到现在。

我（20 世纪）80 年代嫁到篾竹村*去的，我娘家就在篾竹村边上的杨家村，是隔壁邻居呢。以前村里有合作社，编好的竹器由供销社通过船运出去卖。那时私人不能做买卖，本地人要篮子了，就编好给他，他给两斤粮票，算是等价交换。我结婚时候买的竹躺椅，就是婆婆用两条肥皂换来的。

我们摆摊的时候东西都是去竹器师傅家里要的，你要什么跟他说，他愿意做就做，不高兴做就说没有这个东西。也有自己做但不出来卖的，不是每个人都高兴出来卖的呀，那就帮他卖。以前四角篮几毛钱一个，就几分钱利润。现在买的人少了，基本是些前几年的老关系，品种也越来越少，都没东西可供应了。

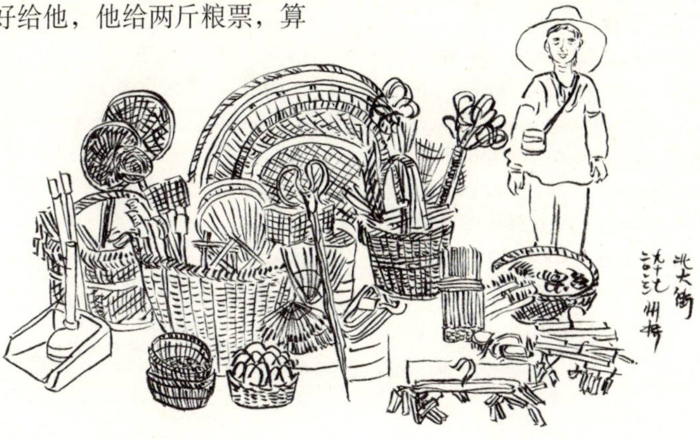

Yang Qiuling: There is few people are willing to do handicrafts now

Everything will be sold out eventually, like circular baskets, four-corner baskets, grain sifters, rice sifters, luo (baskets with a square base with a circular top) and so on. Because few people are willing to make handicrafts now. In the old days, there were about 5 or 6 shops selling bamboo wares in Zhou Qiao. Now, only my shop is left. This stall was originally set up by my grandma. 20 years ago, she passed away. So I resigned from the factory and came to take over the stall.

In the 1980s, I was married and moved to Miezhu Village *. My hometown Yangjia Village (the village of family Yang) was the next to Miezhu Village. In the old days, we had cooperations in the villages. Finished bamboo wares were shipped to other places to sell and all the trading would be operated by the cooperations. At that time, individuals were not allowed to do business. If a local person wanted a basket, we would exchange the finished basket for the Grain Tickets (tickets equal to 1 kilo of rice). Before my wedding, grandma bartered a bamboo armchair in return for two soaps. The bamboo wares we sell here are sourced from the shifu's house. We will tell him what kind of crafts we need. Sometimes he will make it if he has the will of doing and sometimes he will tell us there is no such craft if he is not willing to do it. There are also some people who make bamboo wares but don't sell them as not everyone likes to do business. So we sell on their behalf. In the past, one four-corner basket would cost a few pennies, with only a few cents of net profit. Nowadays, the demand becomes much smaller and most orders are from some regular customers. Also, there are fewer and fewer products which are available to sell.

* Miezhu Village: The name "Miezhu Village" dates back to the late Ming and early Qing dynasty. The village specialized in bamboo weaving and was located in the southern par of Jiading, nowadays renamed as Zhongfang Village, Malu Town

Yang Qiuling, born in Shangahai, 1955
Aug. 2013, Jiading Town, Jiading District

店

杨阿姨的摊位
Ms. Yang's stall

036
篾席
bamboo mat
(for sleeping on)

丁维昌：打（编）一条席子，从破篾开始要八十个小时

老早（以前）篾席都是人家买了竹头，去人家家里做的呀，一套家什（工具）带了到处跑的。现在呢一般都是定做，要么过来买。

打篾席的竹头是黄苦竹，安吉那边买来的，冬天买来我就开（砍）好了，老早生活（活儿）多的时候，过年初一就编了，要不然来不及。现在一般的话4月份开始。打（编）一条席子，从竹子破篾开始，要八十个小时，每天早上7点钟做到夜里6点钟。

十四五根竹子可以打一条篾席，大概要700根长的篾。开竹，拉篾，刮篾，编，锁口，锁好口篾席可以卷起来，放在干燥通风的地方储存。用之前要用开水浇一浇，用开水泡过之后呢，要在阴头里晾干，用起来（篾）韧性足，就不容易断了。篾席要铺硬板床，睡五十年也没问题。

篾席上面梅花、狮子戏球、福禄寿喜图案和文字都可以编的，这个功夫就大了。我跟着师傅五十多年，师傅教的就是平常一般的（基础），自己去看，去试验，最后还是要靠自己的创意。

丁维昌，1944年生于上海
2018年6月，金山区，张堰镇

Ding Weichang: It takes 80 hours to make a sheet or mat from bamboo stripping

In the old days, a craftsperson would make a mat at the customer's house. The household bought the bamboo, and the craftsperson would bring a set of jiashi tools with him or her wherever he or she went. But today we make it according to customers' orders, and some customers will come to the shop to buy it.

The bamboo we use for mie mat is Huang Ku bamboo bought from Anji. I would split the bamboos right after I bought them in winter. We had lots of orders at that time so we would start weaving as early as the first day of the Chinese new year, otherwise we'd finish behind the schedule. Nowadays we start this project in April. It takes 80 hours to make the bamboo strips into a mats, we kick off the working at 7 am and end at 6pm .

It needs 14 to 15 pieces of bamboos to make one mat and that's roughly a total of 700 pieces of mie, the bamboo strips. Split and stripped, the mie will then be stretched, scraped and weaved into a mat. After the open endings is locked up, the mat will be rolled up and stored away in a dry and well-ventilated place. Beforc using the mat, we need to pour some boiling water into it and make it dry in a shady spot just in case it is broken easily. Mie mats are suitable for spread on hardboard beds, which can be used for 50 years.

We can weave all kinds of patterns onto the mat, such as plum blossom, lions playing a ball, characters like fu (prosperity), lu (high position), shou (long life) and xi (happily married), but it needs one's wonderful skill. I followed my Shifu (master) for over 50 years, and all he taught was the basic skills. We have to learn it by watching and testing by ourselves, and above all, we should be creative.

Ding Weichang, born in Shangahai, 1944
Jun. 2018, Zhangyan Town, Jinshan District

丁师傅的工作间
Mr. Ding's workshop

编篾席
making bamboo mat

浦阿婆：现在戴表的人年纪大的多一点

我原来在上海手表二厂工作，退休了就在这里摆个摊（学院路），二十几年了，只要不落雨，我都在。早上 8 点左右（出摊）到下午 4 点左右收摊，半导体（收音机）一天开到晚的。老早（以前）是做修表的人少，要修表的人多，现在么反过来了。

修表的工具有放大镜、镊子等等，小盒子里面放的是零件、机芯，机械表上用的，还有线圈，是电子表里用的。电子表比机械表修得快一点，电子表是很准的，但是不能受潮，受潮了要短路的呀。机械表如果有样东西卡在里面，那就要拆开来，用汽油洗，再一点点装起来，这样就费时间。机械表如果平时不戴的话，起码一年要开个两次，开足，让它走一走动一动，一直放着它也要不舒服的。

我们原来厂里的牌子是宝石花，“两级表”叫银花，就是机器内部好的外观有一点瑕疵，价格也便宜一些。过去买只表要凭票的，都是亲戚的亲戚，朋友的朋友来打招呼，“帮我弄一张票子哦”。我是工作了多少年才分到一张两级票，自己买了戴着。老早（以前）每个人都有表的，现在戴表的人年纪大的多一点。

浦阿婆，1935 年生于上海
2015 年 7 月，黄浦区，学院路

Ms. Pu: Now, the people who wear watches are mostly older people

I used to work at Shanghai No.2 Watch Factory. I came to set up a stall here (Xueyuan Road) after I was retired. It's been more than 20 years since then. I usually work at the stall from about 8am to 4pm unless it rains.The radio is on all day long. In the past, there were few shifu fixing watches, but many watches needed to be repaired. Nowadays, the situation is reversed.

The tools to fix watches include magnifying glasses, tweasers and so on.There are some repair parts and cogs of mechanical watches in this little kit, but coils are used to repair electronic watches. It's quicker to fix electronic watches than mechanical watches. Electronic watches are more punctual, but they cannot be affected with damp, otherwise they will short circuit. For mechanical watches, if something gets stuck inside, then the watch needs to be taken apart, washed with oil and assembled together. That's why it takes more time to fix. If you don't wear your mechanical watch daily, you need to wind it at least twice a year, and wind it tight. There will be something wrong with it if it can't move around.

There was a brand called Jewel Flower which was deveopled by my former factory. The "second-class" watch was called Silver Flower, which means the same engine inside but the outer appearance is a little scarred.So it would be sold at a lower price. In the old days, we needed a "ticket" to buy a watch. Remote relatives and acquaintances would come and ask "can you give me a ticket?" I was assigned a "second-class" ticket after working for quite some years at the factory, so I bought and wore it. In the past, everyone had a watch. Now, the people wearing watches are mostly older people.

Ms. Pu, born in Shanghai, 1935
Jul. 2015, Xueyuan Road, Huangpu District

张凤仙——亭林镇老人的日常服饰

Zhang Fengxian—Daily wear of elders in Tinglin Town

037
土布头巾
homespun headscarf

038
土布衣服
homespun clothes

039
土布围兜
homespun feeding bib

张凤仙，1942 年生于上海
2013 年 8 月，金山区，亭林镇
Zhang Fengxian, born in Shanghai, 1942
Aug. 2013, Tinglin Town, Jinshan District

040
藤椅
rattan
chair

王根林：学徒时没工钱的，师傅肯教你（就）蛮好了

我家里老早（以前）是卖羊肉的，因为我自己欢喜，27岁就去学扎藤椅。我拜了两个师傅，开始是在江阴（江苏省）青阳镇学的编织，这个学得比较快，一年不到就出师了。但是我不会烤架子（用喷火工具把竹子弯成藤椅的骨架），做的时候总归要去求人家，烦不过，那么就再到苏州去学。烤架子老（很）难的，我学了一年多时间才学会。学徒时没工钱的，师傅肯教你（就）蛮好了。

做藤椅么，就是先（劈）开竹子，再把竹子的节刨掉，然后就是烤架子。我年轻的时候一天里可以烤近二十来个架子呢，现在年纪大了（70岁），只能做七八个。编织要等架子烤好之后才可以弄，用藤皮，要慢慢地编，先编脚，再编面子（坐的地方），然后编椅背上的。编一个么总归要一天，至少八个小时。

一般我就做最常用的藤椅，比如“牛角椅”，靠背像牛角一样弯过来的。我到朱家角三十多年了，只有在夏天时做藤椅，这个夏天我已经扎了二十几把了。其他时间我还是卖羊肉，冬天生意好的时候要六个服务员帮忙呢。

王根林，1944年生于江苏
2014年6月，青浦区，朱家角镇，
北大街367号（歇业）

Wang Genlin: As an apprentice I was unpaid, and I felt honored that my master agreed to teach me

My family sells mutton for living. I went to learn binding rattan chairs when I was 27 and I liked it so much. I had two masters. The first one was based in Qingyang Town of Jiangyin City (Jiangsu Province). I learnt it quickly and finished my apprenticeship within a year. But I didn't learn to scorch the structure (using fire torches to heat up the bamboo and bend it into the basic structure of a rattan chair), so I had to trouble the master to help me every time. That was a hassle. So I went to Suzhou and continued my learning. It is difficult to scorch the structure and it took me more than a year to master it. As an apprentice I was unpaid, and I felt honored that my master agreed to teach me.

When I make a rattan chair, the first step is to split the bamboo, trim the knotuckles out, and then scorch the structure. When I was young, I could make about 20 structures within a day. Now I'm older (70 years old), I can only make 7 or 8 within a day. You can start to weave after you finish the structure, by using the rattan peel. Slow down, weave the feet first, then move to the face (the sitting area)and the back. It takes 8 hours at least to finish weaving a chair.

Normally, I only make the most common kind of rattan chair like the "Ox Horn Chair" named after its curved back as, it looks like a horn. I have lived in Zhujiajiao for more than 30 years, and I only make rattan chairs in summer. This summer, I have already made more than 20 chairs. The rest of the time, I still sell mutton for living. The business is so good in winter that I have to hire 6 helpers.

Wang Genlin, born in Jiangsu, 1944
Jun. 2014, No. 367, Beida Street,
Zhujiajiao Town, Qingpu District (closed)

王师傅工作间
Mr. Wang's workshop

工具
tools

041

草拖鞋

straw sandal

顾月香，1953 年生于上海

2014 年 9 月，嘉定区，徐行镇

Gu Yuexiang, born in Shangahi, 1953

Sep. 2014, Xuhang Town, Jiading District

顾月香——徐行镇的草编阿姨

Gu Yuexiang——Straw weaving auntie in Xuhang Town

042
疏篮
loose weave basket

043
饭篮
rice basket

周宏梅，1934 年生于上海
2014 年 6 月，浦东新区，大团镇

周宏梅：要卖得快么就挑（担子）到乡下去，一家家地喊“篮要不要”

我是 16 岁开始学编篮子的。龙潭村（现车站村）这边有名气的呀，过去有几百个人（编）呢，现在都不做了，钞票也赚不到，都开出租车或者种瓜去了。现在谁用竹头篮子呀，现在都用马夹袋了。十年前用的人还蛮多的，淘米、买菜、洗菜。

做一只篮子呢，就是先把竹子劈成条子，然后再劈篾，接着搞这个梅花眼（编底），然后是编篮壳子，接着么穿口装篮襻(提手)，最后包角，就完成了。

常篮（本地音）用来收（摘）东西呀，豇豆、扁豆、桃子、生梨。遇到收草莓的（种植户），一次会订三五十个（放草莓的平底篮），一个人白天做不完的。我一般都是早上 7 点开始编，有时候忙起来做到晚上 9 点多也有的。要卖得快么就挑（担子）到乡下去，一家家地喊“篮要不要”，一大早出门卖到天黑回来。

Zhou Hongmei: In order to facilitate more sales, I would go to the countryside with baskets and peddle household by household: "Do you want a basket? "

I started to learn basket weaving at the age of 16. Longtan Village (now Chezhan Village) is famous for basket weaving. In the past, there were hundreds of weavers. It's so difficult to make money that every weaver give up the job. They either grow melons or drive taxis. Who uses bamboo baskets now? Today, people prefer to use plastic bags, but 10 years ago, there were still quite a lot of people using bamboo baskets for rinsing rice, shopping groceries and washing vegetables.

To make a basket, first you need to chop the bamboo into strips and then make it into mie (thin strips). After that weave the bottom (the shape of meihuayan, literally meaning the eye of plum flowers) followed by the body of the basket, then make holes and install the handle. Finally, wrap up the pointed corners.

The regular baskets are for fruits, like peaches and pears and vegetables, like beans, peas. Sometimes you come across a strawberry planter, who would ask for 30 or 50 baskets as part of a single order. I can't finish them all in a day. Normally, I start weaving at 7 in the morning.If busy, I have to work till 9 pm.

In order to facilitate more sales, I would go to the countryside with baskets and peddle household by household: "Do you want a basket?" I would go out early in the morning and come back after sunset.

Zhou Hongmei, born in Shanghai, 1934
Jun. 2014, Datuan Town, Pudong New Area

工具
tools

编饭篮
making rice basket

044
小竹凳
small bamboo stool

044

黄发堂：以前就是靠这个东西（生活），现在就是做着玩的呀

我在崇明待了二十多年。我改革开放就到上海来搞竹行了，椅子做得最多。现在么不做了，以前就是靠这个东西（生活），现在就是做着玩的呀。

我是我父亲教我的，学了一两年吧，就是先坐在那里玩呀，看呀。我在崇明带过两三个徒弟，现在全部都打工去了。我们都到安徽拿毛竹的，还有安吉、富阳、宁海我们都去拿的，搭大卡车拉回来。这个毛竹要冬天去拿，现在（夏天）不允许砍的。

这个刨竹节的刀片，都是以前买的，现在都买不到了。这个刀片全国做竹器的都要到我们江西去买，哪怕湖南的、湖北的，随便哪里的。现在做（这个刀片）的人去世了，没有人做了，因为（打铁）打不好。

做一个碗架要三天，而且连着三天都不能下雨，因为没有大棚，要去外面（户外）搞的呀。尺寸我们都是算好的，这个里面有两层，放放小菜、盆子和碗，有门。以前每家每户都用的。

黄发堂，1960 年生于江西
2019 年 7 月，崇明区，中兴镇，
红星村 140 号

做竹凳
making bamboo stool

Huang Fatang: I used to do it for a living, and now it's just for fun

I have lived in Chongming Island for more than 20 years. Right after China's reform and opening up, I came to Shanghai and worked in the bamboo industry. I have made many bamboo chairs. I used to do it for a living, but now I do it just for fun.

I spent about 1 or 2 years learning this craft from my father. I just sat there watching my father and playing with it. I had 2 or 3 apprentices in Chongming and now they are all working in the city. We usually source moso from bamboo from Anhui Province, or Anji, Fuyang, or Ninghai (areas of Zhejiang Province), These moso bamboos are only available in winter. In summer, bamboo cutting is prohibited.

I bought this planer blade (used to trim bamboo knots) long time ago, and you can't get one like it now. Every craftsman who makes bamboo wares would come to my hometown in Jiangxi and get this kind of blade, some of whom even come from Hunan, Hubei or anywhere far away from Jiangxi. Now, the man who made this blade is dead. No one could make it, because they don't know how to forge iron well.

It takes 3 days to make a cupboard, and it must be 3 consecutive fine days, because we make them outdoors without awning. The size is confirmed in advance. There are two layers inside the cupboard, and we usually put small dishes, plates and bowls into it.It also has doors. Every household used to have a cupboard like that.

Huang Fatang, born in Jiangxi, 1960
Jul. 2019, No. 140, Hongxing Village, Zhongxing Town, Chongming District

黄师傅的竹行
Mr. Huang's bamboo shop

徐巧珍：天冷的时候，人家都来补羊毛衫、羊绒衫、滑雪衫

我阿爸13岁从乡下（江苏省泰州市）出来，在凤阳路黄河路当学徒，做织补的生活（活儿），过去我阿爸补真丝的旗袍多一点，现在旗袍也没人穿了。(20世纪）90年代我们搬到舟山路，当时这里是马路市场，卖衣服的、洗衣服的什么都有。那时时兴穿西装，全毛料作（衣料）的西装蛀了只小洞，就拿过来补。后来西装不流行了，都是补羊毛衫、T恤衫。

补的时候，要用到放大镜，单凭眼睛看不行的。针么用的是织补针，粗点的么补补羊毛衫，细的呢补真丝。平纹、人字纹（布料的经纬纹路）好弄，斜纹稍微难点，最难的是纹路不规则的料作。

每年到了9月底开始是旺季，一直到第二年的5月份。天冷的时候，人家都来补羊毛衫、羊绒衫、西装、大衣、滑雪衫。

来我这里年纪轻的多，拿来的衣服都是有牌子的，有点小洞还可以补一补再穿。我也碰到过旧的衣服，像老早（以前）这种牙签纹的料子，现在都不流行了，但是人家说是自己结婚时候穿的衣服，要留着做纪念，不是衣服贵要补，对他来讲有价值有意义的，也会来补的。

徐巧珍，1955年生于上海
2015年6月，虹口区，舟山路

Xu Qiaozhen: On cold days, people come to mend their woolen sweaters, cashmere sweaters and ski jackets

My father came here (from his hometown of Taizhou, Jiangsu province) at the age of 13, and worked as an apprentice of tailoring work on Fengyang Road and Huanghe Road. In the past, my father mostly mended silk Qipao (traditional Chinese dress), but nobody wears them anymore now. In the 1990s, we moved to Zhoushan Road. At that time, there was a street market selling clothes and other sorts. Suits were very popular, so many people ask us to mend their woolen suits if they had a little hole eaten by moths. After suits grew out of fashion, we got mostly woolen sweaters and T-shirts for mending.

A magnifying glass is a necessity for mending, because we can't see well with the naked eyes. We use darning needles for mending, the big one used for woolen-wears, the thin ones used for silken-wears. Plain weave or herringbone's fabrics is easy to weave, twill weaves' fabric is a little bit hard. The most difficult one is the fabric with irregular patterns. Every year, the busy season comes around the end of September. In the cold winter, people come here and ask me to mend their woolen sweaters, cashmere sweaters, suits, coats, ski jackets, etc.

Most of my customers are young people. The brand clothes they baing for mending can be worn longer. For the old clothes, like this one which has a toothpick pattern and which is not popular anymore. But the owner said he wore it at his wedding and that's so memorable for him. Someone came here and got the clothes mended, not because of the high price, but because of the significance.

Xu Qiaozhen, born in Shanghai, 1955
Jun. 2015, Zhoushan Road, Hongkou District

织补
darning

045
热水瓶竹壳
thermos flask
with bamboo
casing

046
竹篮
bamboo
basket

竹壳坊

竹兰头

黄金善——住在河边的竹编师傅
Huang Jinshan—— Bamboo weaving Shifu who lives by the river

045

046

黄金善，1939 年生于浙江
2012 年 10 月，青浦区，朱家角镇
Huang Jinshan, born in Zhejiang, 1939
Oct. 2012, Zhujiajiao Town, Qingpu District

047
草编东方明珠电视塔
straw-plaited Oriental Pearl Tower

048
南瓜包
straw bag

049
草帽
straw hat

047

甘丽娟：以前家里的开销都是靠草编，现在是大家开心了一起弄弄

草编我小的时候跟爷爷、奶奶、妈妈都学过。我一开始在徐行毛巾厂工作，草编都是加工做的呀，都是业余做的，厂里上班我们是三班制的，那么我们日里（白天）上班，夜里回来就可以在家里做草编。假如中班的，那么我们日里在家里做草编。

（草编用的）黄草以前我们都是每家每户种在自留地里的，清明节后落籽（播种），到了7月份就可以拔草了。甪直（江苏省）那里他们种黄草的也会撑船把草带过来卖给我们。

（20世纪）70年代出口都是做包。包的造型么草编厂会拿打样（样品）来，发给农村里的人，大家一面种田，一面就做草编。都做一样的，颜色也是一样的。厂里规定你怎么做就怎么做，做好了么卖给草编厂。做得不好的也要退回来的，退回过来的就没用了。到了（20世纪）90年代，转成做出口拖鞋了。

现在还有几位七八十岁的在编，主要是为了解解厌气（解闷）。以前家里的开销都是靠这个的，现在叫作是大家开心了一起弄弄。

甘丽娟，1950年生于上海
2013年7月，嘉定区，上海工艺美术职业学院，工艺美术研究中心

Gan Lijuan: In the past, we earned our living by making straw wares, but today we just do it for fun when we get together

I learned straw plaiting from my grandparents and mother when I was a kid. At first, I was working in Xuhang Towel Factory and only did some straw plaiting in my spare time. The factory ran on 3 shifts, for example, if we were working in the daytime, we could make straw wares when we got home in the evening. If we were working in the evening, then daytime was available.

In the past, every household would plant yellow straw (used for straw plaiting) in their own backyards. As we sowed right after the Qingming Festival (Tomb-Sweeping Day, in Spring), we would reep during July. People from Luzhi(Jiangsu province) would also come here by boat and sell their yellow straw.

During the 1970s, the main products of export were bags. The straw plaiting factory would give samples of bags to the people in the village. When we took a rest from farming, we made bags of the same style and color. We followed the guidelines from the factory, because the bags were sold back to them. If the quality didn't reach the standard, the bags would be sent back and considered to be scrapped.

When it came to the 1990s, slippers became the main products for export. There are only a few old people around (70 to 80 years old) who are still doing this craft now, mostly to entertain themselves. In the past, we earned our living by making straw wares, but today we just do it for fun when we get together.

Gan Lijuan, born in Shanghai, 1950
Jul. 2013, Crafts Research Center, Jiading
Shanghai Art & Design Academy,
Jiading District

048

049

050
竹篮子
bamboo
basket

051
竹蜻蜓*
bamboo
dragonfly*

*竹蜻蜓：竹制儿童玩具，由形似蜻蜓双翼的螺旋桨和细轴组成，用双手快速搓揉细轴放飞
* bamboo dragonfly: a children's toy made of bamboo, composed of a propeller in the shape ofdragonfly wings and a thin axis, it flies up when one rubs the axis with speed

朱金林，1948 年生于上海
2013 年 7 月，青浦区，朱家角镇
Zhu Jinlin, born in Shanghai, 1948
Jul. 2013, Zhujiajiao Town, Qingpu District

050 朱金林——会做竹蜻蜓的杂货店主

Zhu Jinlin——A houseware store owner who can make bamboo dragonfly (a flying toy)

做竹蜻蜓
making bamboo dragonfly

051

十月的小荡
Xiaodang Village in October

052
铜手炉
copper hand-warmer

殷允良——在公交站旁卖日用杂品
Yin Yunliang——Runs a variety store by the bus stop

殷允良，1961 年生于上海
2019 年 11 月，黄浦区，人民路 19 号
Yin Yunliang, born in Shanghai, 1961
Nov. 2019, No. 19, Renmin Road, Huangpu District

052

053

竹匾*

bamboo bian*

王秀丽——我卖杂货有七十年了

Wang Xiuli——I have been selling groceries for 70 years

053

竹篾扎脚架

竹匾

王秀丽，1923 年生于上海

2019 年 12 月，徐汇区，陕西南路 249 号，东兴丝网竹器商店

Wang Xiuli, born in Shanghai, 1923

Dec. 2019, Dongxing Wire Mesh and Bamboo Ware Shop, No. 249 South Shaanxi Road, Xuhui District

*匾：用竹篾编的圆形扁平盛物器具

*bian: a flat round split-bamboo basket

054
蟹篓
crab basket

055
草莓篮
strawberry
basket

沈友高，1944 年生于上海
2013 年 10 月，金山区，枫泾镇

沈友高：以前么每户人家总归有人会做（竹编）

以前么每户人家总归有人会做（竹编）的，现在我们村里一直在做的，也就四个人，基本在 70 岁左右，也是想着做了就做，岁数大了身体（体质）跟不上了呀。

我十三四岁就开始学了，就这样看着人家做，拿两根篾自己编编就会了。做完了拿到街上去卖，基本都是一早四五点出门，到附近的镇，（比如）枫泾、蒸淀、练塘，骑的总归（一定）是永久的重磅车，把两根竹子插在脚踏车后面，串个三十多只篮子，很高的呀。

现在我一般早上 4 点半就起来了，5 点钟到枫泾镇上面的茶馆里喝茶，8 点回到家里开始干活。我们的房子刚造好三年，这间本来是当车库的，我就专门用来编编篮子了。我会编箩，抓鱼用的；长箩，钓黄鳝用的；还有食堂里洗菜用的河篮（音），比一般的箩还要大呢，都是食堂里要了，叫我做再做，他们不要，自己做了也卖不掉的。每个人都有自己的刀，我 16 岁打（定做）了把，后来用到快磨断掉了，就换了这把刀，也是叫人定做的，这把用掉（坏）么，我也做不动了。

Shen Yougao: In the past, every household had someone who could do bamboo weaving

In the past, every household had someone who could do bamboo weaving. There used to be about 50 to 60 weavers in our village, but now there are only 4 people who are still doing it, and they are mostly around 70 years old. Because of their old age, they do it only when they feel like it.

I started to learn bamboo weaving when I was 13 or 14 years old. After watching other people weaving, I practised weaving two bamboo strips and mastered the skill.After I finished my products, I would take them to the street to sell. Normally I went out at 4 or 5 o'clock in the morning and the destination is usually the nearby towns like Fengjing, Zhendian, Liantang. I always rode a heavy Forever (Chinese brand) bike. I would fix 2 pieces of bamboo on the back of the bike and string up more than 30 baskets. They would be stacked so high.

Nowadays, I get up early at 4:30 am and go to the tea house in Fengjing Town around 5:00 am. Then I come back home and start working at 8:00 am. Our house was built 3 years ago and it's quite new.This room was supposed to be the garage and now I make baskets in it. I can make luo (with a square bottom and a round mouth) which is used to catch fish. Longluo for fishing finless eels. The helan (river basket) is bigger than the normal luo, which people use to wash vegetables at the canteen. I only make it when the canteen people have the demand. Otherwise I won't make it, because it is difficult to sell. Everyone has a knife of their own. I had my first tailor-made knife when I was 16, which was all rubbed and almost broken. Now I get this new one which is also custom-made.When this knife is worn out, I will quit my job.

Shen Yougao, born in Shanghai, 1944
Oct. 2013, Fengjing Town, Jinshan District

晒草莓篮
drying strawberry baskets

编草莓篮
making strawberry basket

056
小篮
small basket
056

俞锦仙：我编的小篮子，来古镇旅游的外国人看到都要买的

我现在这间屋子，是专门用来编篮子的。老早（以前）这里编篮子的人多，现在少了，我算是这里做的（篮子）花样多的。老早村里有人在做，我就边上跟着做，就是看来的，没有师傅教的。

毛竹一般都去竹行买，一次买10～20根，自己开电瓶车拖回来。我一般都是连续劈一天的篾，把要用的料子准备好。毛竹粗的一头，可以劈好了做篮子，细的梢子呢，就用来做档手，有的么缘口用的，很细的篾专门用来做小篮子，都不一样的。一般一根竹子可以劈4～8层，10层也有的，要看编什么东西。

工具我这边多了，很多别人都没有的，因为我做的东西（品种）多。这个木墩子，用来削（竹子）的，是我自己做的。还有刮篾用的工具，刀是买的，架子我自己做，老早打篾席要用的。

我平时做做小的筻，洗菜用的篮子，还有匾、筛子、竹子扶梯，样样都做的，在镇上开店的都问我订货，还有两百来只等着（做）呢，尤其我编的小篮子，来古镇旅游的外国人看到都要买的，好玩呀，每天这种小的篮子可以做二十个。

俞锦仙，1940年生于上海
2013年10月，金山区，枫泾镇

Yu Jinxian: My handmade small baskets are popular even among the foreigners visiting the old town

This room is especially for basket weaving. In the old days, there were many basket-weavers in the town. When they were making baskets in the village, and I just stood aside and watch them. I learned the craft in that way instead of learning from shifu (master). Now there are far fewer basket-weavers. I am probably one of the makers here who know about most designs.

Moso bamboos are usually bought from the bamboo shops, 10-20 pieces by once. I carry them back by electric bike. Normally, I work continuously for a day, chopping bamboos into mie (thin strips) and preparing all the materials. The bulky end of a moso bamboo, after being chopped, can be used to make baskets; and the thin end of the bamboo can be used to make the handle. And some thin strips are used to make the collars or mini baskets; they're all different. Normally, a bamboo is chopped into 4 to 10 strips, depending on what kind of stuff you are making with it. I have many tools here, but many people don't have these, because I need to make more designs. This wooden stool is used to peel bamboo, which I made by myself. This tool is used to trim bamboo strips. I bought the knife, but the holder is handmade by myself. In the old days, these tools were used to make bamboo mats.

I often make small-sized Da (bamboo mat used to dry grains and tea leaves), baskets for washing vegetables, and also Bian (a flat round split-bamboo basket), sifters, bamboo stairs, etc. I make all kinds of stuff, and all the shopholders in the town, place orders from my shop. I still have 200 baskets waiting to be made, especially the mini-baskets I made. They even caught foreigner's eyes who visited the Old Town, such as these mini-baskets. I can make about 20 ones per day.

Yu Jinxian, born in Shanghai, 1940
Oct. 2013, Fengjing Town, Jinshan District

057
铁锅
iron wok

058
铁勺
iron spoon

059
铁铲
iron shovel

陶情建——马路边的铁榔头

Tao Qingjian——Iron hammer by the road

陶情建，1960 年生于上海
2014 年 10 月，虹口区，舟山路
Tao Qingjian, born in Shanghai, 1960
Oct. 2014, Zhoushan Road, Hongkou District

060
棉花胎*
cotton quilt padding*

*棉花胎：棉花制成的被褥内芯

*cotton quilt padding: the filler of a duvet, made of cotton

唐师傅：我大概是弹棉花里面年纪最轻的了

我 16 岁从兰溪（浙江省）到上海来弹棉花，弹了三十年了。我是跟我哥学的，学的时候，总归要敲到两只手肿起来才会，我用了半年时间才弹得像点样子。老早（以前）我们十几个弹棉花的，在曹家渡租房子住在一起，都是我们老家的人，现在有些年纪大了就不做了，我大概是里面年纪最轻的了。

弹一床棉花胎，要一个多钟头（小时）。一开始么就是把（旧棉花胎）外面的纱拆掉，然后把棉花撕小，就开始弹了。弹松了就铺平，一面上好纱后把它翻过来，再弹另一面，最后用（木）盘把纱和棉花捻在一起。刚弹好的棉花胎要垫在床上压一下，棉花就不会松开来，大概要垫一个礼拜，有太阳么拿出来晒晒，不过一定要先垫。

我背着的工具叫弹弓，是木匠师傅做的，大概有六七斤重。除了大热天（夏天）休息，天气好的时候我都会出来弹。人家打电话我就来了，都是预约的。一般早上 7 点出门，晚上做到 5 点钟，这两天比较晚，要弄到 7 点钟。昨天一户人家拿出来五条（棉花胎），我总归要帮人家做完的。

唐师傅，1968 年生于浙江
2014 年 9 月，长宁区，茅台路

Mr. Tang: I am probably the youngest among the cotton-fluffing craftsmen

When I was 16 years old, I left Lanxi (Zhejiang province) and came to Shanghai to do cotton-fluffing. It has been 30 years since I learnt the skill from my elder brother. I kept practising until my both hands swelled. It took me half a year to master the basic skill. In the old days, there were a dozen of us, all from my hometown, doing cotton-fluffing, and we rented a house in Caojiadu and lived together. Now some of us have grown old and stopped doing it. I am probably the youngest among them.

It takes more than an hour to fluff a paddin. First, you take off the gauze (of an old padding), then you tear the cotton into small pieces and start fluffing it, until it's loose and fluffy again. Then you flatten it and put on a gauze. Then you turn it over and fluff the other side. At last, you use a wooden plate to make the gauze and the cotton stick together. A freshly fluffed padding needs to be pressed and padded on a bed, so the cotton won't loosen. You pad it for about a week. On sunny days, you take the padding out to sunbathe, but you must pad it first.

This is a fluffing bow that I am carrying on my back. It's made by a carpenter, and it's about 3 to 3 and a half kilos. Unless it's a very hot day, I always come out to work. Customers usually call me-my work has been arranged in advance. I often leave home at 7am and finish my work at 5pm. I worked till a bit later these days. Yesterday, I finished 5 paddings within in a day for one customer.

Mr. Tang, born in Zhejiang, 1968
Sep. 2014, Maotai Road, Changning District

弹棉花
cotton-fluffing

陈天星——新场大街的白铁匠

Chen Tianxing ——Iron Forger in Xinchang Street

061
漏斗
funnel

062
舀水勺
water spoon

063
铅桶
lead bucket

064
油墩子勺*
youdunzi spoon*

065
畚箕
dustpan

陈天星，1943 年生于上海
2014 年 11 月，浦东新区，新场镇，新场大街 207 号
Chen Tianxing, born in Shanghai, 1943
Nov. 2014, No. 207, Xinchang Street, Xinchang Town, Pudong New Area

*油墩子勺：白铁制成的椭圆形勺子，用于油炸一种内有萝卜丝的面粉食品
*youdunzi spoon: a deep-fried pie stuffed with meat or turnip

061
063
062
064
065

066
小元宝篮
small yuanbao basket

元宝篮子

王全林：嘉定这里用得最多的还是元宝篮

我会编四角篮、圆篮、元宝篮、淘米篮，还有小的布篮，老早（以前）家里织布用（来放小东西）的。筛子、食堂里用的菜箩也编，大大小小都有的。嘉定这里用得最多的还是元宝篮，样子弯弯的像个元宝一样，老早么就用来买小菜、收收地里种的东西（菜）。马陆不是种葡萄嘛，他们摘葡萄都要用（元宝篮）的。

我从小就做这个了，祖传的呀，父母都做这个的，靠这个吃饭的，最早是在自己家里编。以前我们村（众芳村）里家家户户都编的，每个人会编的都不一样，基本都会三四样东西。老早都是自己在乡下做好，然后带到集市上去卖。或者带个四五十只篮子，骑自行车到十六铺，摆渡去浦东、川沙卖。后来个人不可以做了就去生产大队里做。现在大家基本都不做了，后头一代更加不会做了。

我么现在住在新房子里，在最高层，地方大得不得了，就在走道或者阳台里编，高兴做就多做点，不高兴么就少做点。摆摊的阿姨经常来问我要篮子啊筛子什么的，我来不及做，还有其他地方的人也来跟我定做，不单单是嘉定的。

王全林，1947 年生于上海
2014 年 10 月，嘉定区，马陆镇

Wang Quanlin: The most popular basket in Jiading is still the yuanbao basket

I can make quadrangular baskets, circular baskets, yuan bao baskets shoe- shaped gold ingot, rice-washing baskets and small fabric baskets, which we use to put odds and ends when weaving fabrics. I also mkc sifter and vegetable baskets big and small, used in the canteens. The most popular one is still the yuanbao basket in Jiading, curved like a gold ingot. We used to carry it when we went shopping in a grocery store or picked vegetables in the fields. People in Malu use yuanbao baskets for picking grapes.

I began to do that when I was a kid. It is a craft passed down from the old generations. My parents also made their living by doing that. In the beginning, we weaved at home. In our village (Zhongfang Village), every household used to make baskets, and everyone knew different styles, but they could all make at least 3 to 4 different of baskets. In the past, we made the baskets at home before going to the market. Or we rode a bicycle with 40 to 50 baskets, stopped at Shiliupu Dock and took a ferry to Pudong, and went to Chuansha to sell them. Later, individuals were not allowed to make and sell baskets, so we went to work in a factory. Now, almost nobody does it anymore, certainly not the next generation.

Now, I live in a new flat on top of a bolck with a large space. So I weave baskets in the corridor or on the balcony. I can make more when I feel in the mood, but sometimes I make fewer when I am not in the mood. The aunties selling things at the stalls often ask me for baskets and sifters, but I don't have enough time to meet their demands. I also get orders from places outside Jiading.

Wang Quanlin, born in Shanghai, 1947
Oct. 2014, Malu Town, Jiading District

066

编元宝篮
making yuanbao basket

067
迷你三轮车
mini tricycle

068
迷你脚踏车
mini bicycle

查沛华：我做的脚踏车都是可以转动的，跟真的一样

我老早（以前）是在皮革厂做皮鞋的，大概是 1987 年的时候，在静安公园门口有个老头在做这个(迷你脚踏车),很多人围着看，我也很感兴趣。那时他八十几岁了，看看我的手指头那么粗，又是弯的，也没答应要教我。后来我下岗了，认识了一个“小安徽”（安徽人）也是做这个的，就买他的东西回去研究，2008 年的时候我开始自己做这种脚踏车。

做一部车子要两百多个动作呐，我眼睛不好，手指头也不好，脚也不好，又要设计又要做，还要自己去采购材料，还要到马路上去卖。一开始做出来的东西歪歪扭扭、长长短短、七歪八气的，过了几年，做的东西总算可以看看了。我做的脚踏车都是可以转动的，跟真的一样。有英国的蓝羚，（国内的）永久、凤凰，除了脚踏车还有三轮车、老爷车、黄包车。

现在我夜里么闭门造车，日里(白天）就出来摆摊头，每天卖掉哪个，我回到家里还要做一个，保证第二天出去卖的时候各种品种都要有的呀。这里经常有外国人来拍照，有时还要给人家指指路，因为我的摊头摆在马路边嘛。

查沛华，1951 年生于上海
2015 年 9 月，静安区，江宁路

Zha Peihua: All the bicycles I have made are rotatable like real ones

I used to be a shoemaker at a leather factory. Around 1987, there was an old man over 80 years old making these kinds of mini bicycles in front of Jing'an Park. He was surrounded by people watching him, including me. I was so interested in it. But he felt that my fingers were too thick and bent, so he did not teach the skills to we. Then later, I was laid off from the factory and got to know Little Anhui (a young man from Anhui Province) who was also doing this craft. So I bought some bicycles from him and studied them by myself. From 2008, I began to make this type of bicycle by myself.

It takes more than 200 steps to make one bicycle. I had poor eye sight, and my fingers and feet were not strong enough for this business.But I did every step one by one, from design to making, from purchasing raw materials to selling the products on the street. At first, the bicycles I made were crooked and twisted and some were longer while some were shorter. After a few years of making, they were finally presentable. All the bicycles I made are rotatable, like real ones. I made models of Raleigh from the UK, Forever and Phoenix (both are Chinese bicycle brands), and tricycles, and vintage cars, rickshaws.

Usually I work at home in the evening, and come out to sell in the daytime. If one model is sold, I will make a new one after I go back home. I need to make sure every different kind of model is available the next day. Foreigners often take photos around my booth; sometimes I show people the way, because my booth is right on the street.

Zha Peihua, born in Shanghai, 1951
Sep. 2015, Jiangning Road, Jing'an District

067
068

商品信息
棉花胎 每斤 28.00元（新疆棉花）
金狮牌地板蜡 每包 15.00元（沪产）
蟑螂屋、老鼠粘板、蚊香、电蚊拍、
各式热水瓶 热水瓶胆、
管道疏通剂 食用碱、去污粉、洁瓷精
瓶胆除垢灵、尼龙躺椅、竹片躺椅、各种痰盂
各式行李车、购物车有售、

秦师傅：我们卖的东西大概有近千种吧

我们这家店新中国成立前就开在襄阳南路了，现在店员有八个人，卖的东西大概有近千种吧，基本都（摆）放出来了，都是一些家庭日用品。门口的黑板报是店里的师傅写的，根据季节的转换和进货的信息，写在上面给大家看看，常卖的东西我们都有备货的。顾客的话除了附近的居民，还有大老远跑过来买东西的，慕名而来的人，也有外国人来买的。

每次店里盘好货后就可以知道什么卖得好，哪些快卖完了，赶快去进，哪些是老百姓需要的，就要去找。我们有几个店员，下午三四点后他们进店，上午都是各自在外面找货源，比如今天客人来要个什么，如果没有的话，他们得去想办法找到。

现在天还没到最最冷的时候，卖得最好的是棉花胎。棉花胎我们一年四季都摆出来的，天热的时候就放薄的，冬天就放厚的，按斤数（每床的分量）来的呀。其他像热水瓶配胆什么的，还有铁锅子最好卖。以前腌东西的坛子、陶罐、竹壳热水瓶现在不卖了，有些是大家不使用了，或者就是产品更新换代了。煤球炉还有货，但现在用的人很少很少了。

秦师傅，1960 年生于上海
2018 年 11 月，徐汇区，襄阳南路 223 号，南方日用品商店（歇业）

Mr. Qin: We sell about a thousand items here

We opened this shop before liberation, right on South Xiangyang Road. Now, we have 8 shop assistants, and sell about a thousand items. They are almost on display, most of which are daily necessities. The blackboard at the doorway is updated by a shop assistant. Based on the change of seasons and new arrials,the information of our items need to be updated, so we write it on the board so that people can see it. For the most frequently sold items, we have extra stock. Customers are mostly the people living nearby. There are some customers who come from far away. Some customers come for the reputation of our shop including some foreigners.

Every time after we check the inventory ventory, we know which items sell well. If one item is almost sold out, we need to purchase more; and we need to sourte the items in great need. We have a couple of assistants who arrive at the store at about 3 or 4pm, and in the morning, they usually look for the items on their own. For example, if a customer would like to buy something that we don't have, then these people need to find it.

It's not yet the coldest time of the year, but the bestseller is usually cotton blankets. We have cotton blankets every season of the year. In summer, we sell the light ones, and in the winter the heavy ones. It's measured by jin (half a kilo). Other stuff, like the flask refills and the iron pots, are also popular. We used to sell pickle jars, pottery pots and flasks in bamboo casing, but not anymore. It depends on the customer demand or they are replaced by products upgrading. We still have coal stoves, but few people use them now.

Mr. Qin, born in Shanghai, 1960
Nov. 2018, South Daily Goods Store, No. 223, South Xiangyang Road, Xuhui District (closed)

南方日用品商店内
inside South Daily Goods Store

069
迷你茶壶
mini teapot

070
迷你汤婆子*
mini hot water bottle*

071
迷你手炉
mini hand-warmer

069

*迷你汤婆子：内灌热水的取暖用具，一般放在被窝里暖脚，迷你汤婆子为工艺品
*Mini hot water bottle: artware, usually made of copper, to warm with filling of hot water. Here mini warmer is souvenir

夏耀明，1948 年生于上海
2015 年 11 月，奉贤区，四团镇

夏耀明：南京路、城隍庙都有卖我（做）的东西

我现在做这个算铜艺制作，是兴趣爱好，没有多长时间，大概三五年。我年轻时在大团镇上的村办厂里面做机修工，也做钣金、电镀，基本都是机械方面的工作。当时没有师傅，就是在厂里自己钻研弄弄，厂里买了各种设备，就到人家厂里去学习学习。

制作材料有紫铜、黄铜、白铜，我要自己跑到上海（市区）买回来，顺便也去白相（玩）一下。工具么就这些呀，钻床、车床、抛光板和榔头啊这些小工具。步骤么一开始么落料呀，然后压料、钻孔、焊接、抛光、装环。现在忙的时候我儿子他么也来帮忙做做。手炉、脚炉、汤婆子，这样一套叫“迷你嫁妆”，南京路、城隍庙都有卖我（做）的东西。

我读书读到高小，看书看得多，初中里的平面几何、立体几何，还有机械制图的书都要看的，主视图、俯视图、左视图、右视图，因为做这个东西，你基础知识要有一些的。不懂的地方就是要学，自己学，没有师傅。

Xia Yaoming: You can find the things I made in the stores on Nanjing Road or around Chenghuang Temple

This is a kind of a copper craft that I am doing, my hobby, and I only work in this area for about 3-5 years. I used to be a mechanic in the village factory of Datuan Town, doing metal plating and electroplating, mostly related to machines. At that time, there was no shifu (master), so I studied by myself. The factory bought all sorts of equipment and I would go to other factories to learn.

Materials are needed to make such pieces include red copper, brass and cupronickel. I would need to go to downtown to buy these materials, so I would take the chance to have fun in the city on those trips. As for the tools, here they are: drill press, lathe, polishing spanner, and small tools like the hammer. The process is as follows first blanking, then pressing, drilling, welding, polishing and ring fixing. Nowadays, my son also comes to help me when I get busy. We have what we call a "mini dowry kit": a hand-warmer, a foot-warmer, and a general warmer (tang pozi). You can find the things I have made in the stores on Nanjing Road or around Chenghuang Temple.

Though I didn't have more education after primary school, I know a lot of things, for example, basic plane geometry usually taught in junior high school, and books on mechanical drawing (CAD), front view, top view, left and right elevation, and so on. For grasp of this craft, you need some basic knowledge. I keep learning when I see something fresh and I am both a master (shifu) and a apprentice.

Xia Yaoming, born in Shanghai, 1948
Nov. 2015, Situan Town, Fengxian District

070
071

做迷你嫁妆
making mini dowry

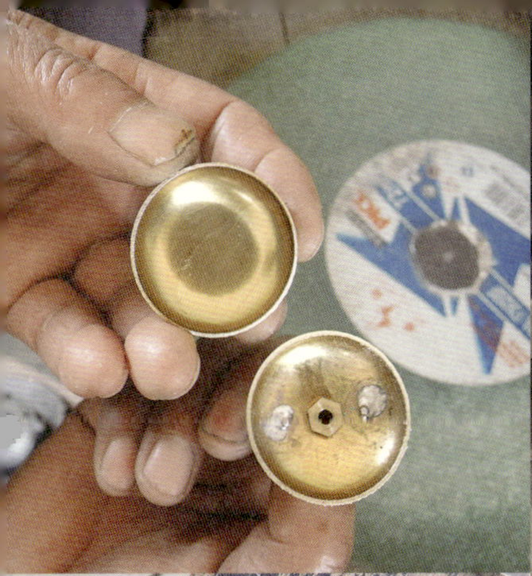

072
土布鞋
homespun
cotton shoes

华雪娟，1954 年生于上海
2013 年 10 月，奉贤区，奉城镇
Hua Xuejuan, born in Shanghai, 1954
Oct. 2013, Fengcheng Town,
Fengxian District

华雪娟——平安镇织布阿姨

Hua Xuejuan——Weaving auntie in Ping'an Town

073
铁鎝*
iron rake*

073

*铁鎝：有三到五个铁齿的翻土工具
iron rake: rake with three to six teeth, it is an agricultural tool for ploughing

朱阿梅——在胡桥镇打农具

Zhu Amei——Forging agricultural tools in Huqiao Town

其他农具
other farming tools

朱阿梅，1947 年生于上海
2018 年 9 月，金山区，胡桥镇
Zhu Amei, born in Shanghai, 1947
Sep. 2018, Huqiao Town, Jinshan District

074
皮拖鞋
leather slippers

徐文鸿，1943 年生于江苏
2019 年 11 月，黄浦区，康家弄

徐文鸿：带不了徒弟，不吃生活（教训）学不会

这个鞋铺摆了近十年了，老早（以前）有十几个品种，现在平时就做拖鞋、布鞋，农历十月份还做棉鞋。来买的都是年纪大的，中国台湾人、外国人，还有住在嘉定（区）、宝山（区）的。有的几十双一买。

从早上 7 点到晚上 7 点，一天做三双吓死人了（撑足了）。鞋子尺寸从 37 码做到 46 码，鞋楦我都有，37、38、39，这些呢要的人顶（最）多。小孩的，要定做了。鞋底以前是布头的，现在布头的鞋底谁来扎啊，后来还有塑料底的，现在是橡胶底的。老人为了防滑，会特地要做橡胶底。拖鞋是皮底的。

我 16 岁就到上海来了，老家在江苏扬州，之前在家种田。我师傅是我爸，我学了一年。我爸教过五个徒弟。他以前还做绣花鞋什么的，缎子的，难多了。我没带徒弟，有人要学的，我不教。带徒弟不吃生活（教训）学不会。

Xu Wenhong: Apprentices need to be lessoned, otherwise they would not learn

This shoe shop has been here for almost ten years. In the old days, there were a dozen different kinds of products. Now we only make slippers and cloth shoes, and in October of the Lunar calendar, we also make cotton-padded shoes. The customers are mostly elder people, including foreigners, people from Hongkong and Taiwan, and those who live in Jiading (district) and Baoshan (district). Some custowers even bought dozens of pairs of shoes.

I work from 7 in the morning till 7 in the evening, and I can make 3 pairs of shoes a day at most (which is amazing). The sizes range from 37 to 46, and I have all the shoe trees, amoug which 37, 38 and 39 are the most popular sizes. For kids, their shoes need to be specially made.

The soles used to be made of cloth. Nowadays, nobody sews cloth soles. At one point there were plastic soles, and today we make rubber soles. Afraid of slipping, the old people in particular often ask for rubber soles. And for slippers, we make leather soles.

I came to Shanghai when I was 16. My hometown is Yangzhou, (Jiangsu Province), and I used to do farming. My Shifu is my father, from whom I learnt for one year. My father had five apprentices. He also used to make embroidered shoes, satin stitched and all sorts; those crafts were much more difficult to learn. I have no apprentices. There were some people who asked me to teach them, but I turned them down. Apprentices need to be lessoned, otherwise they would not learn.

Xu Wenhong, born in Jiangsu, 1943
Nov. 2019, Kangjia Lane, Huangpu District

做皮鞋、修皮鞋
making leather sandals, repairing leather shoes

075
扫帚
broom

075

费宝英：我还是比较喜欢卖传统的东西

店门口这些小牌子写了二十二年了，我这边地方小，很多商品没办法摆出来，所以就写在小牌子上挂在外面，有上千种，让人家知道我这里什么都有。外国人路过我这里都跷大拇指的，他们还撑着三脚架拍照，也不晓得我的店有什么好玩的，他们就说我有创意。

店里一般都是我一个人，我老公么在外面进进货、送送货。我跟他说呢，进货你千万别进那种便宜的、看不上眼的东西，总归进的东西要考虑我自己可以用伐，你说对嘛，这样我跟别人介绍东西也底气足了。

像现在天冷么，痰盂罐卖得蛮好的，还有蛤蜊油、百雀羚、永字老牌热水袋；春天到了，店里就会进一点传统的樟脑丸；夏天折扇也很好卖的，上次有个老先生来买了五把，说一个房间放一把，省得跑来跑去。附近小学开学的时候么，书套卖得比较多了，还有铅笔套、卷笔刀，钢笔也有的，我都卖英雄（牌）的，英雄钢笔，我还是比较喜欢卖传统的东西。

假如说以后不做生意了，我肯定是画画、写字、弹钢琴，还有结绒线，我比较喜欢文艺点的。

费宝英，1951 年生于上海
2019 年 10 月，徐汇区，太原路 126 号，昊诚商行

Fei Baoying: I prefer to sell traditional things

It has been many years since I first wrote and hung up these tags in front of the shop. My place is small and lots of products can not be displayed. So I use these small tags and display them outside, so people can know what I sell here. There are 50 to 60 kinds of commodities. Foreigners passing by always give me a thumb up, and they even set up tripod and take photos. They say it's so creative, even they if don't know my shop well.

I am often in the shop alone. My husband is usually out, purchasing and delivering the goods. I always tell him to ensure the high quality of and the goods to think first if it would be good enough for our own use. Right? So I am confident when I sell them to customers. Now it is cold so spittoons sell well, so do clam oil, Pechoin and the Yong hot water bottles (an old classic brand). When spring comes, we will stock with some traditional items like mothballs. Folding fan is a good seller in summer. The other day, an old man came and bought 5 folding fans, one for each room, he said, so there was no need to bring the fan around. When the nearby elementary schools open, we sell a lot of book covers, pencil cases and sharpeners. I also sell pens, but I always sell Hero (Chinese brand) pens. I kind of prefer to sell traditional things.

If I don't do business anymore in the future, I'd like to paint, write, play the piano and knit. I like to make my life colorful.

Fei Baoying, born in Shanghai, 1951
Oct. 2019, Haocheng Housware store,
No. 126, Taiyuan Road, Xuhui District

昊诚商行内
inside Haocheng housware Store

一月的渔池
Yuchi Village in January

王师傅背着做锭子（纺车上的零件）的工具
Mr. Wang is carrying tools for making spindles (a key part of a loom)

王雪根：每匹布都有名字，我能叫得出几百种

我 18 岁开始学做锭子（纺车上用的），还有织布的梭子，19 岁出去卖锭子、梭子，修纺（纱）车、（织）布机。老早（以前）都是踩脚踏车，最远我跑到过嘉定（上海市郊）。当初浦东这边学这个手艺的有 200 个人，到现在只有我一个人了。不要看我是老伯伯，我也会纺纱织布的，因为我这个锭子给（帮）他们（顾客）加工了之后，要试做给他们看好不好用。纺纱车和织布机都是木匠做的，而且是老手艺的木匠才会做，一般做家具和造房子的木匠不做的。这个跟我们搓锭子的一样，是专行。

我也不是一直都在搓锭子，当中因为有洋布了，所以自己纺纱的人也少了，我就做别的事情去了。到了 50 岁才开始收集土布，基本上都是从浦东和崇明地区来的。布头的花色大概有好几万种，每匹布都有自己名字，我能叫得出几十种、几百种，全部叫得出不可能的。有句老话叫“织不完的布样子，讨不完的巧娘子”。裁缝呢是我“80 岁学吹打”——到老了才刚开始学起来的。店里这些衣服、旗袍都是我做的呀，不过我一个人做不过来时，也会找其他老裁缝一起做。现在我的儿媳妇也帮我做做。

王雪根，1950 年生于上海
2013 年 1 月，浦东新区，新场镇，新场大街 448 号

Wang Xuegen: Every piece of fabric has its own name, I can recognize hundreds of them

I started to learn how to make spindles and shuttles when I was 18, and one year later, I began to sell the spindles and shuttles I made, and to repair spinning wheels and looms. In the past, we all rode bicycles and the farthest place I had been to was Jiading (a suburb of Shanghai). At that time, there were around 200 people learning this craft in Pudong, but now I am the only one left. You may think I am an old man, but I can do spinning and weaving too, because when I sell the spindle I need to make some samples to show the clients the spindle's good quality. Spinning wheels and looms are all made by carpenters who must know the traditional craft and techuique. Those carpenters who make furniture or decorate houses can not make them. It is a specialized trade.

I haven't been making spindles all my life. When machine-made fabrics became available, fewer people were using spinning wheels so I went to do something else too. It wasn't until I was 50 that I started to collect homespun fabrics, which mostly came from Pudong and Chongming Island. There are tens of thousands of different kinds of designs and colors, and every piece of fabric has its own name. I can recognize hundreds of them, it is impossible to recognize them all. As an old saying goes: endless patterns to weave, countless smart young ladies to marry. And I only started to learn to be a tailor when I got old (as the saying goes: one starting to learn wind and percussion instruments at 80 can easily be out of breath). I made all these clothes and qipaos. But when there are too many orders and I can't manage them all, so I have to ask call other old tailors for help. Now my daughter-in-law also comes to help me.

Wang Xuegen, born in Shanghai, 1950
Jan. 2013, No. 448, Xinchang street, Xinchang Town, Pudong New Area

二〇一四、八、二

076
鹤
red-crowned crane

077
蟹
bamboo crab

078
小藤匾
small bamboo tray

079
大崇明篮
big Chongming basket

郭志高：我用的都是崇明的土竹

我的竹编手艺是家里祖传的，我 18 岁开始跟爸爸学，到现在已经编了五十年了。之前在生产大队集体做过，当时一起编的有三五十个人，现在就我们几个了。我编点小东西用的都是崇明的土竹，在我家旁边就有个竹林，要用了就砍一点。我手上这把竹刀，用了起码二十年了。

篮子便当（容易），一天可以编三个。筛子做起来复杂，小筛子，眼子（孔）小的，功夫大，一个白天还做不完呢，要开夜工才能做好。这地上有（画了）两个圈，就是用来做匾的尺寸。这个小匾里面有个“喜”字，要一天人工。编其他字也可以的，“福”“自力更生”都可以编。字的颜色是我自己染的，颜色染好么就用手工编出来。

定做也可以，你只要带张图纸来，留个电话号码，做好么我打给你。现在定做的人蛮多的，我们镇上的文化馆也来我这里定做，这次定的是要编一个仙鹤，编了好几天了，我还会编鱼、毛蟹这种，都是用来演戏的道具。一般我都在家里编，偶尔也去上海（市区）参加一些（民间手艺）活动。

郭志高，1944 年生于上海
2014 年 11 月，崇明区，城桥镇

Guo Zhigao: I always use the local bamboo from Chongming for the small things I made

My bamboo weaving craft is handed down from my family. It has been 50 years since I started to learn the skill from my father when I was 18. I used to do it at the production brigade with 30 to 50 people; only a few of us are still doing it today. I always use the local bamboo from Chongming for the small things I make. There is a bamboo forest near my house, so I just go out and cut some down whenever I need it. This knife in my hand has been used for 20 years at least.

It is easy for me to fiuish three baskets within a day. Sifters are more complicated to make, especially the smaller ones with small holes-they take a lot of effort, and you have to work day and night. These two circles drawn on the ground are used to measure bian (a flat, round split-bamboo basket). The Chinese character inside is "xi" (meaning happy marriage) which takes a day to weave. Other characters are also fine, like "fu" (good fortune) and "zili gengsheng" (be self-reliant). I dye the characters by myself. When I've finished dyeing, I weave it.

I can also make special bespoke orders. Just bring me the pattern you want and leave a telephone number, and I will call you when it is done. Nowadays, there are quite a lot of special orders and even the town cultural center comes to find me. Recently they have ordered a bamboo crane, which I have been waking for several days. I can also make fish and crabs, which are for performance props. I usually weav at home. Occasionally I attend some folk craftsman events in Shanghai.

Guo Zhigao, born in Shanghai, 1944
Nov. 2014, Chenqiao Town,
Chongming District

077

078

079

080

连枷*

flail*

*连枷：用于油菜，麦子，黄豆等农作物脱粒的工具

*flail: an agricultural tool for threshing grains and beans

顾振邦——向化镇
竹器摊主

Gu Zhenbang——
A bamboo ware stall seller in Xianghua Town

顾振邦，1950 年生于上海
2015 年 1 月，崇明区，向化镇
Gu Zhenbang, born in Shanghai, 1950
Jan. 2015, Xianghua Town, Chongming District

081
崇明土布
Chongming homespun

082
聪明羊
smart sheep

083
土布帽子
homespun sunhat

084
土布包
homespun bag

何永娣：我出嫁的时候布就是自己织的

崇明以前有十万台（织）布机之说呢，每家每户都有的。我出嫁的时候布就是自己织的，我织了八块，不同的花色。现在本地50岁以下的都不会织了，我结婚后就没织过。

记得是上幼儿园那时候就看妈妈织布了。妈妈不是织布的时候会配色嘛，多下来的线头妈妈会给你看，让你跟着她一起学配色，小时候就是从配色开始学起。妈妈说要经纱（织布的工序）了你去看啊，上（织布）机了你去看怎么上的，这样一步步（过程）。我十五六岁的时候就可以织一块完整的布出来了。

因为织过布，知道织布的辛苦，二十年前我开始收集土布，现在有两万多种花型，五百多类。常见的有蝴蝶布、梅花布、路路通、井字布、斜纹布……花头（花样）都是劳动中创作的，你找不到两匹布是一模一样的。我在尝试把织布的手艺，结合到学校教育中，像种植物、种棉花，纳入了语文课、数学课、自然课、英语课中；染色呢纳入化学课中；织布机的杠杆原理纳入物理课……从小学一年级到初中三年级。

何永娣，1971年生于上海
2018年2月，崇明区，向化镇，永春村493号，永娣土布传承馆（需预约）

He Yongdi: The cloth for my wedding was weaved by myself

It has been said that in Chongming there used be a hundred thousand weaving machines. Every household had one. The cloth for my wedding was weaved by myself. I weaved 8 pieces with different colors and designs. Now people aged under 50 do not know how to weave. I stopped weaving after I got married.

I remember watching my mom weaving when I was still in kindergarten. She needed to match the colors as she wove. She would show me how to use the leftover bits and pieces, and ask me to learn from her how to match the colors. That's how I started, simply from color matching. Mom used to say it was time for warping (a step before weaving), and I had to watch it, or it was time to start weaving, and I should watch how. Just follwing that, I learnt these skills step by step. At the age of 15 or 16, I could weave a complete piece of fabric. Because I weaved and I know the hardship of weaving 20 years ago, I started to collect homespun fabrics. Now, I have about 500 different kinds of fabrics with 20,000 patterns. The common ones include butterfly mesh, plum flower, basket weave, glen plaid, and twill The patterns were all hand-made so you cannot find two pieces of fabrics with the same design. I try to incorporate the craft of weaving into schools' education programs. For example, cotton plantation can be incorporated into Chinese, math, science and English classes; coloring can be incorporated into chemistry classes and the principle of levers used in the weaving machines can be incorporated into physics. These can be learned in classes from Grade 1 in primary school to Grade 9 in junior widdle schools.

He Yongdi, born in Shanghai, 1971
Feb. 2018, Yongdi Homespun Fabrics Museum, No. 493, Yongchun Village, Xianghua Town, Chongming District (by appointment)

织布机
weaving loom

085
棕绷*
zongbeng*

*棕绷：用棕绳穿成的床铺
*zongbeng: a mattress made of palm fiber

周万德：我自己也是睡棕绷的，透气

我是十几岁开始学生意的，做了一辈子棕绷。过去我伯伯有个店叫“周羲泰棕绷号”，开在平济里路（现济南路），我就跟他请来的同乡老师傅学。过去上海滩上有两三百家棕绷店，阿拉（我们）江西丰城来开棕绷店的最多，属于“西帮”，江苏人呢叫“苏帮”，还有本地人开的棕绷店，叫“本帮”。后来睡棕绷的人少了，店就逐步逐步没了。

刚开始学的时候，师傅做什么你就跟着一起做，还有几个师兄，有的专门搭架子，有的专门穿棕绷，有分工的。穿棕绷比我有名气的人也有的，但是像我这样会搭架子，穿（棕）线，做棕绷、藤绷，能做全套的不太有。平时阿拉还帮人家做修理。一年四季当中，5 月份到 10 月份生意最忙。现在的季节（12 月）早上 7 点开始做，到晚上四五点，太阳落山了回去。很辛苦，你看，手指头特别粗，像胡萝卜一样。

北方干燥，不适合用棕绷；南方么潮湿，棕绷越是潮湿寿命越长。这个做棕绷呢暂时也不会失传，只要有人用就有人做，我自己也是睡棕绷的，透气。

周万德，1956 年生于江西
2014 年 12 月，黄浦区，东台路 112 号

Zhou Wande: I myself sleep on a zongbeng bed (with a wooden structure and a surface woven with palm fibers); it had better ventilation

I started to learn the business in my teens, and I have been making zongbeng beds in my whole life. In the past, my uncle had a shop called "Zhou Xitai's Zongbeng" on Pingjili Road (now Jinan Road). I learned the skill from an in-house master, who came from the same village as us. In the past, there used to be two or three hundred zongbeng stores in Shanghai. We came from Fengcheng, Jiangxi Province, and we are called the "Xi Clan", the biggest clan. The makers from Jiangsu Province were called "Su Clan", and the local stores were called "Local Clan". Later, fewer and fewer people slept on zongbeng beds, and the stores gradually disappeared.

When I started learning, I just followed and copied the master. There were a few senior apprentices, someone specialized in making the structure, and someone specialized in weaving the surface with palm fiber threads. There were also some people famous for weaving the surface, but there are few like me who can do the whole set of making the structure, weaving the threads, making both palm and rattan beds. On a normal day, I also help fix broken beds. Throughou the year, it is the busy time from May to October. In this season (December), I start working from 7am till 4 or 5pm, and go home at sunset. It's a very hard job as you can see from my fingers, which are as thick as carrots.

It is dry in the north (Northern China), and it is not suitable to use a zongbeng bed. In the south, it is wet and in the wet surroundings the zongbeng lasts longer. Now I think the skill of making zongbeng shouldn't be lost. As long as there are still people using them, there should be people making them. I, myself, sleep on a zongbeng bed-it has better ventilation.

Zhou Wande, born in Jiangxi, 1956
Dec. 2014, No. 112, Dongtai Road, Huangpu District

做棕绷
weaving zongbeng

两位师傅一起做棕绷
two masters are making zongbeng bed together

手織

居台仁——老师傅的小板凳

Ju Tairen——Old Shifu's small stool

086

居台仁，1950 年生于上海
2019 年 12 月，嘉定区，徐行镇
Ju Tairen, born in Shanghai, 1950
Dec. 2019, Xuhang Town, Jiading District

087
兔子灯*
rabbit lantern

陈志刚——老城厢里的小师傅
Chen Zhigang——Young Shifu in the old town

087

手工兔子灯

陈志刚，1971 年生于江苏
2013 年 2 月，黄浦区，豫园，方浜中路 386 号
Chen Zhigang, born in Jiangsu, 1971
Feb. 2013, No. 386, Middle Fangbang Road, Yuyuan Garden, Huangpu District

*兔子灯：元宵节时儿童玩的兔子形状的纸花灯
*rabbit lantern:a paper lantern in the shape of rabbit for children at Lantern Festival

088
菜刀
chopping knife

089
田刀*
rake*

090
篾刀*
mie shaving knife*

*田刀：用于翻土松土的工具
*rake: tool for tillage
*篾刀：劈制竹篾的刀
*mie shaving knife: used to chop bamboo into thin strips

张福平：我就做做当地农民用的农具

我出生在大团，是1966年开始学打铁的，在大团铁业社，我师傅姓汤，带了五六个徒弟。我们每天7点上班一直工作到下午4点，八个小时，中午休息。老早（以前）我们有一百多个人呢，都是从大团各个地方来的。就做割稻子的镰刀，还有铁鐇、挖河沟的槽刀（音）、菜刀，都是农具，老早农作需要的东西比现在多。

我从单位退休回来就在家里做了。打铁的工具都是自己做的，比方讲钳子、铁锤。打铁先是落料，放在1000（摄氏）度的炉子里加热后，在生铁做的铁墩子上头锻打，这是打铁最难的工序。然后是蘸火（淬火），反复几次，打成所要的农具的形状，成形后再打磨、抛光，然后就完工了。

我也带过五六个徒弟，后来都不做了，要么转行要么退休了。我就是做这个工种熟练呀，再做别的工种，重新学起来也不高兴了。来这里买东西的也都是当地农民，我就做做他们用的农具，老早篾匠师傅用的竹刀也打的，就是现在要得少，一把两把打起来烦不过，现在我每天可以打二十把菜刀。不过现在割稻什么的都用机器了，不需要人工和那些工具了呀，所以打铁的人也越来越少了。

张福平，1950年生于上海
2015年1月，浦东新区，大团镇

Zhang Fuping: The regular customers are local farmers; and I forge farming tools for them

I was born in Datuan Town, and I started to learn forging in 1966, at the forging station in Datuan. My shifu was Mr. Tang, and he had about 5 or 6 apprentices. Every day, we started working at 7am and finished at 4 pm; 8 hours in total including a break at noon. In the old days, we had more than 100 people, coming from different region of Datuan. We mostly made farming tools, like sickles for reaping wheat, cramp irons, slot drills for digging river ditches, chopping knifes for kitchen use and so on. In the old days, farming activities required more tools than today.

After I was retired, I started to do it at home. I made the forging tools, such as pliers and hammers by myself. Forging iron requires the following steps. First you need to heat up the metal in a stove at 1,000 degrees, then you forge it on a foot stool made of crude iron, which is the most difficult step. Then you douse it with water. You repeat the above steps a few times, shaping the metal into the farming tool you are making. After it takes shape, you polish and shine it, which is the last step.

I also had 5 or 6 apprentices, but they all quit eventually-someone turned to other businesses, while others were retired. I am experienced at this skill, and I feel reluctant to start a new business. Most people who come to buy stuff here are local farmers, and I make farming tools for them. In the old days, I also made bamboo knives for the mie master (who makes bamboo wares). Since there is low demand now, it would be troublesome if I only make one or two knives for once. Now I spend most of the time forging chopping knives and I can make about 20 knives every day. Today, people usually use machines to cut rice, and there is no more need for field helpers and hand tools. So fewer and fewer people come to forge tools.

088

089

Zhang Fuping, born in Shanghai, 1950
Jan. 2015, Datuan Town, Pudong New Area

做篾刀
making mie shaving knife

090

张师傅和他妻子及孙子在他的工作间
Mr. Zhang in the workshop with his wife and his grandson

091

土布

homespun

091

储进根，1939 年生于上海
2015 年 2 月，浦东新区，新场镇，
新场大街 224 号
Chu Jingen, born in Shanghai, 1939
Feb. 2015, No. 224, Xinchang Street,
Xinchang Town, Pudong New Area

储进根——在新场镇卖老杂货

Chu Jin'gen—Selling old wares in Xinchang Town

储师傅的杂货店
Mr. Chu's general store

092
生肖灯*
zodiac lantern*

*生肖灯：元宵节时儿童玩的十二生肖形状的纸花灯

*zodiac lantern: paper lanterns in the shape of the 12 zodiac animals for children at the Lantern Festival

李建国：老客户有的年年要来买一个生肖彩灯

我是本地人，阿拉爷（爸爸）倒不喜欢做这个东西（彩灯），我爷爷会做，我也算是传承了祖辈的手艺。老早（以前）本地逢年过节传统气氛比较浓，要扎龙灯啊什么的，我爷爷是川沙镇上做彩灯比较老举（拿手）的。

做一个彩灯要五六个小时，我平时要上班，一天就做一两只东西，像麒麟这种造型比较复杂的要做一个礼拜。我这里比较有特色的是十二生肖的彩灯，这些造型我会先画出来，再照着样子做。我的职业是电工，但从小欢喜画画，人家都在弄堂里打弹珠玩，我么就在家里画画。

我在这里（丽园路）摆摊子快七年了，习惯了，一般年初一开始摆到正月十五元宵节。本来我住在这里附近的，后来搬到浦东去了，现在从家里过来要三刻钟。来买的很多是老客户，有的年年要来买一个生肖灯，也有来定制大型彩灯的。每年我总归要做300～500只彩灯，平时就把零件都做好，然后到时候再扎起来，一步步拼装。有一年啊，我做了一房间的兔子灯，结果卖不掉，人家都买塑料的了。现在不一样了，反过来了，都要买手工的了。

李建国，1956年生于上海
2015年2月，黄浦区，丽园路

Li Jianguo: Some regular customers come to buy a zodiac lantern every year

I am a native. My father was not interested in lantern-making, but my grandfather was different from him. So you can say I inherit the craft from the old generation. In the old times, folk traditions were very popular, and when it came to festivals and new year, we made dragon lanterns and some handmade goods. My grandpa was a top maker of colorful lanterns in Chuansha town.

It takes about 5 to 6 hours to make a colorful lantern. I work on weekdays, so I can only make about 1 or 2 lanterns per day. This lantern of unicorn shape is complicated, and it will take about a week to finish. My specialty is the lanterns of 12 zodiac animals. I draw the sketches first and make the lanterns accordingly. My job is an electrician, but I like drawing so much, since I was young. When the other kids were playing marbles in the longtang (small alleys), I was drawing at home.

I have been selling the lanterns at this stall (on Liyuan Road) for about 7 years. Usually, I come to the stall at the begining of the lunar new year and stay here and sell until the day of the Lantern Festival. I used to live nearby, but I have moved away to Pudong New Area, so it takes about 45 minutes to get here from home. Most buyers are regular customers and they come to buy a zodiac lantern every year. People also come to buy tailor-made giant lanterns. I make about 300-500 colorful lanterns every year. I often finish the parts earlier and when it comes to the appropriate time, I just asseable the parts together, One year, I made a whole room of rabbit lanterns, which were not sold at all, because people went to buy plastic ones. Now, the situation has changed-it's reversed-everyone likes handmade ones again.

Li Jianguo, born in Shanghai, 1956
Feb. 2015, Liyuan Road, Huangpu District

李师傅做的兔子灯
the rabbit lantern made by Mr. L

Jumen Rd
便利

093
匾*
bian*

吴孝明——城桥镇的竹编师傅
Wu Xiaoming——Bamboo weaving Shifu in Chengqiao Town

吴孝明，1941 年生于上海
2016 年 2 月，崇明区，城桥镇
Wu Xiaoming, born in Shanghai, 1941
Feb. 2016, Chengqiao Town, Chongming District

*匾：用竹篾编的圆形扁平盛物器具
*bian: a flat round split-bamboo basket

094
木盆
wooden buckets

杨忠岐——七宝镇上的木桶匠
Yang Zhongqi——Wooden bucket maker in Qibao Town

094

杨忠岐，1946 年生于江苏
2013 年 2 月，闵行区，七宝镇，徐家弄 22 号
Yang Zhongqi, born in Jiangsu, 1946
Feb. 2013, No. 22, Xujia Lane, Qibao Town, Minghang District

095
饭窠*
fanku*

096
长颈鹿
straw-plaited
giraff

095

*饭窠：用稻草等编制的保温饭菜的用具
* fanku (meal cover): a straw-plaited cover to keep meals warm

沈木云：老早（以前）每家人家都要用饭窠的

我十一二岁的时候看着爸爸做，有时候爸爸去吃饭去了，我就偷偷地学着做。大概十六七岁的时候吧,（水平）跟爸爸差不多了。爸爸是跟爷爷学的,妈妈也会做。老早（以前）我们白天在地里做生活（活儿）,夜里回来吃好晚饭，就开始做这些东西。

老早的饭窠我们都是用稻草来做的。现在这里是茭白之乡，稻草也没有了，有的话也是收割机割的，原来都是人工割稻的，割的稻长，不容易断掉。现在从 5 月份到 10 月份这段时间，茭白叶子一直都可以摘的。刚刚摘下来要太阳里暴晒三天，晒干了之后要拿尼龙布扎紧，要密封，挂起来。用茭白叶编饭窠的过程是：整理（茭白叶的长短）,绕芯（编扎底部）大约五圈，盘边（一圈圈盘起高度）大约八圈，收口。

像老早上海人烧煤球炉,先烧饭，再烧菜,烧菜不是饭要冷掉了嘛，就放在饭窠里保温，每家人家都有的，专门到这里来买的。现在条件好了呀，有草（饭）窠也不用了，有电饭煲了。

沈木云，1956 年生于上海
2019 年 1 月，青浦区，练塘镇，
朱枫公路 3516 号

编饭窠
making fanku

Shen Muyun: In the old days, people in Shanghai used coal stoves to cook, and every household had a fanku to keep their cooked rice warm

I started to watch my father making this fanku (a container to keep cooked rice warm) at the age of 11 or 12. When he went for meals, I would secretly learn to do it myself. When I was 16 or 17 years old, I almost could make it as well as my father. My father learned it from my grandfather, and my mother could also do it. In the past, we worked in the field in the daytime and came back in the evening for dinner, then right after eating we started to make these things.

We used to make fanku with straws Today, the fields which were used to grow straw has been used to plant zizania latifolia, so there is no more straw. Even if there is any straw, it is reaped by machine. Previously, we would reap it by hand and the straw would be cut long, so it was not easy to break. Nowadays, zi zania latifolia are always available from May to October. Their freshly picked leaves need to be exposed in the sun for 3 days, then wrapped up tightly in nylon cloth after getting dry, then sealed and hung it up. The procedure of weaving fanku with such leaves is as follows: sort out the leaves by length, weave the bottom by going around the center about 5 rounds, weave the side by going upwards about 8 rounds, and close up.

In the old days, people in Shanghai used briquette stoves to do cooking, and they would cook the rice first, then the dishes. When the dishes were done, the rice would be naturally cold, right? That's why people put the rice in a fanku to keep it warm. They were commonly used in every household and people would come here to buy them. Now, life get better, we use electric cookers instead of fanku. So it's difficult to find any more fanku in the market.

Shen Muyun, born in Shanghai, 1956
Jan. 2019, No. 3516, Zhufeng gong Road, Liantang Town, Qingpu District

097
藤拍*
rattan racket*

098
小藤椅
small rattan chair

周伟清，1969 年生于上海
2019 年 12 月，浦东新区，大团镇，永辉小区 3 栋 6 号，永晖藤器店

*藤拍：晒完被子后，用于拍打被子的用藤条编制的用具
* rattan racket: a rattan-weaved racket used to beat duvets

周伟清：在上海，藤椅没有几个人在做了

我 1985 年进大团的藤器厂，做了有三十多年了。刚进厂的时候十几岁，学起来蛮快的，做做看看呢，就慢慢会了。我们一道进厂的小青年有好多呢，后来他们有的做做就不做了，离开了。我一直做到藤器厂关掉，就自己出来做了。

所以我又会做（藤椅的）架子，又会穿（藤椅的面）。有的人只会做架子，穿么穿不来的，有的呢穿会穿，架子做不来的。当时年轻么，师傅呢叫我做架子，那么我就做架子，做架子的人多了，那么我就去穿了。就这样搞搞弄弄么都会了。

做藤椅先要腾料作（准备材料）——竹梢和藤皮。料作腾好么断料——把竹梢按尺寸锯好，然后用火烤架子——把竹梢烤成弯的，烤骨架定型是最难的一步，再穿藤皮，编藤椅的面。藤皮都是从印尼那边来的。从头到底，每个步骤都我一个人做，一日天要的。现在么一般都是我搭架子，我老婆帮忙穿，在上海，藤椅已经没有几个人在做了。

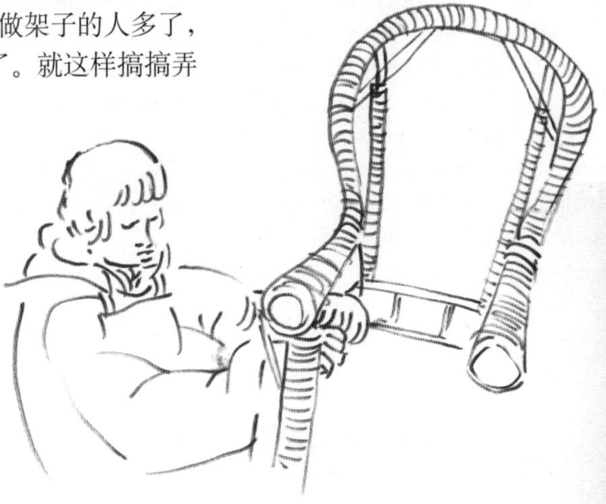

Zhou Weiqing: In Shanghai, there is few people who are still making rattan chairs

I started to work at the rattan-ware factory in Datuan Town in 1985, and I worked there for more than 30 years. When I was still a teenager , I joined in and was quick at learning. Through watching and practice, I gradually learned the craft. There were a lot of young people who started out as a maker with me together. But some of them left after a while. I had been working at the factory until it was closed. Then I came out and worked as an independent trader.

I can both make the structure and thread the face (the surface) of rattan chairs. Some people can only make the structure, but not the face, and some the other way round. At that time, I was young, and when Shifu asked me to make the structure, I learned it. When there were too many people making the structure, I was asked to thread the face. Then after a while, I learnt all the craft of making rattan chairs.

To make a rattan chair, first you need to prepare the materials, i.e. the bamboo pieces and the rattan skins. Then, chop the bamboo into set pieces, and make the structure by heating up the bamboo and bending it into a certain shape, which is the most difficult step. Finally, thread the rattan skins and weave the face of a chair. The rattan skins are imported from Indonesia. From the beginning to the end, I used to do everything myself, and it often took a day to finish it. Now I usually set the structure, and my wife can help me to weave the surface.

In Shanghai, there are few people who can make rattan chairs.

Zhou Weiqing, born in Shanghai, 1969
Dec. 2019, Yonghui Rattan Ware Shop, No. 6, Building 3, Yonghui Complex, Datuan Town, Pudong New Area

做藤椅
making rattan chair

永晖藤器店，周师傅的工作间
Yonghui Rattan Ware Shop,
Mr. Zhou's workshop

小簸箕
099
小簸箕
small dustpan
100
大竹匾
large bian
099

黄达明：我每个星期要去学校教小朋友做竹编功课

做笼格（蒸笼）、篮子就是从我太太（祖母）、公公（祖父）这么一代代传下来的。我是跟父亲学的，兄弟里就我学了，哥哥出去工作了，那个时候家家户户会做。现在么就我们几个了呀，其他就算还有会做的人，也就做只篮子，其他一样做不来的。现在高兴么就做做，不高兴么就不做了。我们的下面一代都不做了，做别的去了。

1958年的时候我在崇明竹器厂，主要是做生活日用产品，像笪，晒粮食用的，还有各种农具。工人最多的时候，有三四百人。现在退休了，平时做道具多，崇明有十多样特色道具，羊头、黄金糕、大白菜、花菜、草莓等等，老年大学里的美工画好样子，我用竹子搭好架子，然后上面还要糊纸或者布，演戏用的。簸箕是用（崇明）本地的竹子做的；大一点的匾呢我就用毛竹来做，两种竹子不一样的。

我每个星期要去本地明珠小学教小朋友做竹编功课，三、四、五年级，一次么十五个小朋友，他们聘请我的。还有老年大学、文化馆的民间艺术活动、展览都叫我去展示的。

黄达明，1939 年生于上海
2013 年 12 月，崇明区，城桥镇

Huang Daming: Every week, I go to teach bamboo weaving at a local primary school

The craft of making bamboo steamers and baskets was passed down through the generations from my grandma and grandpa. I learnt from my father, and I was the only one who learnt the craft in my generation and my elder brothers had their jobs. In the old days, every household knew the craft by heart. Now, only a few of us know the craft, and the rest, even if they can do bamboo weaving, can only make baskets and not the other stuffs. Now, bamboo weaving is more like a pastime and I do it when I feel in the mood. Our next generations don't take it at all, and they are engaged in other businesses.

In 1958, when working at the bamboo ware factory in Chongming, I mainly made daily necessities, like da (a flat bamboo sheet used to dry grains in the sun) or other farming tools. In the peak period, the factory had 300—400 workers. Now I'm retired and mostly make performance props. The paintings from the Elderly University (local community school for the retired people) are very good. I make a structure with bamboo, then stick paper or cloth on it. It's used for performance. To make dustpans, I use local (Chongming) bamboo, and to make bian, I use moso bamboo, Which are two different kinds of bamboos.

Every week, I go to teach bamboo weaving at Mingzhu Primary school, a local school, for pupils in Grade 3, 4 and 5, often 15 kids for one lesson. They invite me to teach. Also, when Elderly University and the cultural hall have folk arts events, they always ask me to show my crafts.

Huang Daming, born in Shanghai, 1939
Dec. 2013, Chengqiao Town,
Chongming District

黄师傅的工作间
Mr. Huang's workshop

工具
tools

丰 生
公斤

参考读物
Additional Reading

《日用杂品商品知识》，张正南主编，内部发行，1987 年

《上海手工业史料汇编》，王定一主编，内部发行，1991 年

《中国民居》，王其钧编绘，上海人民美术出版社，1991 年

《上海轶事大观》，陈伯熙编著，上海书店出版社，1999 年

《上海话大词典》，钱乃荣编著，上海辞书出版社，2008 年

《乌泥泾手工棉纺织技艺》，陈澄泉、宋浩杰主编，上海文化出版社，2009 年

《上海生活 1950—2010》，徐步主编，南方日报出版社，2010

《徐行草编》，张德祺主编，上海文化出版社，2011 年

《上海灯彩》，张伟英主编，上海文化出版社，2011 年

COLORS [85] Going to Market——去逛街，2012 年

《留住手艺》《留住手艺 II》，［日］盐野米松著，英柯编译，广西师范大学出版社，2012 年、2019 年

Makers of East London, photograhy by Charlotte Schreiber, Written by Katie Treggiden, HOXTON MINI PRESS, 2015

《上海掌故大词典》，薛理勇主编，上海辞书出版社，2015 年

《日常东京》，［日］都筑响一著，陈怡君译，大田出版，2016 年

《沪乡记事》，沈月明著，生活·读书·新知三联书店，2017 年

《设计探侦》，［日］松田行正著，黄友玫译，漫游者，2018 年

《 MUJI BOOKS 人与物——柳宗悦》，［日］柳宗悦著，杨珍珍译，新星出版社，2018 年

《考现学》，［日］今和次郎著，行人文化实验室，2018 年

1

2

3

4

5

6

7

9

凤阳路
11

13

14

15

16

17

18

19

21

23

25

26

27

28

29

摄影 李恺 Photo by Li Kai

30

1 本书作者 周祺
2 “上海篮子”展览，徐汇艺术馆
3《汉声》杂志北京编辑部
4 日本作家 盐野米松
5 平安镇的阿婆
6 练塘镇河边的杂货铺

7 朱师傅在阮巷市集卖农具
8 手工爱好者杨帆和卖篮的师傅
9 东兴丝网竹器商店王阿婆和她的女儿
10 庄师傅拿着用草编的藤拍
11 老城厢的木作流动摊
12 学生蔡祺跟周师傅学劈篾

13 向化镇竹器摊
14 “上海杂货铺”展览，上海市群众艺术馆
15 平安镇的阿姨们在经线（织布前的准备工作）
16 跟枫泾镇的阿婆去竹编师傅家
17 设计师清水耕助定做的崇明篮
18 设计师刘昊星和设计专业学生许嫣然看郭师傅劈篾

19 七宝古镇的桶店老板娘和老板
20 摄影师中田美佐在新场跟阿婆学用农具
21 王师傅的儿媳在新场土布店里
22 摄影师袁佳青拎着王师傅做的元宝篮和鱼篓
23 和德国汉学教授马可 赫尼格参加法兰克福书展“上海杂货”的论坛
24. 本书翻译 张渊

25 徐行镇盛阿姨自己种的黄草
26 黄师傅坐船从竹行运毛竹回家
27 和魏师傅、马师傅、解阿婆在顺昌蒸笼店
28 中德文化顾问王竞与各国孔子学院院长参观昊诚商行
29 采访南方日用品商店的秦师傅
30 和中文系教授汤惟杰听陶师傅讲如何修补汤婆子

31 作者家中一角
32 “上海竹编”展览，无印良品(杭州)
33“海陆之间——跨大西洋艺术”展，世界文化博物馆（法兰克福）
34 和本书美术指导姜庆共，设计师马德岗，策展人林清在金山
35 本书英文校对之一 白杰
36 南门港的竹篮流动摊位

1 author of this book: Zhou Qi
2 Shanghai Baskets, exhibition, Xuhui Art Museum
3 *Han Sheng*, Beijing editorial department
4 Japanese writer: Yonematsu Shiono
5 a grandma in Ping'an Town
6 general store by the river in Liantang Town

7 Mr. Zhu is selling agricultural tools at Ruanxiang Market
8 a handicraft lover Yang Fan and a basket-selling master
9 Ms. Wang and and her daughter at Dongxing Wire Mesh and Bamboo Ware Shop
10 Mr. Zhuang holding a straw-plaited racket
11 wooden moving stalls in Shanghai Old Town
12 student Cai Qi is learning how to chop bamboo into Mie (thin strips) with Mr. Zhou

13 bamboo-ware stall in Xianghua Town
14 Shanghai Housewares, exhibition, Shanghai Mass Art Museum
15 aunties from Ping'an Town are warping (a prep step before weaving)
16 on the way to bamboo weaving master's house with a local grandma from Fengjing Town
17 Chongming basket ordered by designer Kosuke Shimizu
18 designer Liu Haoxing and a design student Xu Yanran are watching Mr. Guo chopping mie (thin bamboo strips)

19 the wooden basin shop owner and his wife in Qibao Town
20 photographer Misa Nakata is learning how to use farming tools with a local grandma in Xinchang Town
21 Mr. Wang's daughter-in-law at Xinchang Homespun Fabric Shop
22 photographer Yuan Jiaqing is holding some Yuanbao baskets and fish baskets made by Mr. Wang
23 attending Shanghai Housewares forum at Frankfurt Book Fair with German sinologist Marcus Hernig
24 translator of this book: Zhang Yuan

25 yellow grass planted by Ms. Sheng in Xuhang Town
26. Mr. Huang is transporting moso bamboos by boat from the shop to his home
27 at Shunchang Bamboo Steamer Shop with Mr. Wei, Mr. Ma and Ms. Xie
28 German-Chinese cultural consultant Jing Bartz and directors of Confucius Institutes all over the world visiting Haocheng Housware Store
29 interviewing with Mr. Qin of South Daily Goods Store
30 listening to Mr. Tao on how to repair a hot water bottle, with a professor Mr.Tang Weijie

31 a corner of the author's home
32 Shanghai Bamboo Weaving, exhibition, Atelier MUJI (Hangzhou)
33 Entre Terra e Mar-Zwischen erde und Meer transatlantische Kunst, exhibition, Weltkulturen Museum (Frankfurt)
34 at Jinshan District with the art director of this book Jiang Qinggong, designer Ma Degang and exhibition curator Lin Qing
35 one of the book's proofreaders: Jake Newby
36 moving stalls selling bamboo baskets in Nanmen Port

31

32

33

34

35

36

图书版权编目 (CIP) 数据
上海师傅——最后的手作记忆：汉文、英文 / 周祺
编著 . -- 上海：上海人民美术出版社，2020.8
ISBN 978-7-5586-1665-5
Ⅰ . ①上… Ⅱ . ①周… Ⅲ . ①手工业史－上海－现代
－图集 Ⅳ . ① F426.899-64
中国版本图书馆 CIP 数据核字 (2020) 第 075854 号

出品人：顾　伟
统　筹：邱孟瑜

上海师傅
——最后的手作记忆

编　　著：周　祺
责任编辑：张　璎
美术指导：姜庆共
翻　　译：张　渊
审　　校：张柏如
英语审校：张　炜　朱卫锋　白　杰
技术编辑：王　泓
设　　计：周　祺　上海风景工作室
出版发行：上海人民美術出版社
印　　刷：上海雅昌艺术印刷有限公司
版　　次：2020 年 8 月第一版
印　　次：2020 年 8 月第一次
开　　本：787mm × 1092mm 1/32
印　　张：9
ISBN　978-7-5586-1665-5
定　　价：138.00 元

上海市长乐路 672 弄 33 号 / 200040 / 021-54044520 / www.shrmms.com